Brian C

Hunter combat pilot (KIA)

![photo]

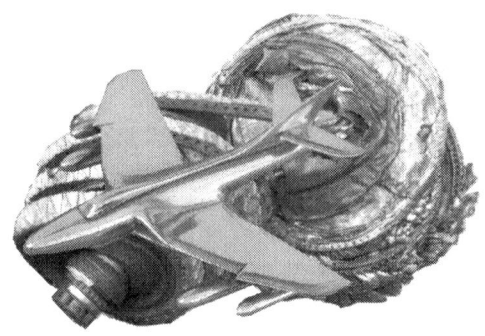

First published in 2008 by Prop Geldenhuys prop@peysoft.co.za

Copyright © Prop Geldenhuys
Design and origination by Prop Geldenhuys of Peysoft Publishing
Back cover Op Uric map © Dr JRT Wood

ISBN: 978-0-359-31178-1
KDP ISBN: 9781792621321
eBook ISBN:

Paeroa
2018

†

Dedicated to the memory of a

bold combat pilot killed in action

during Operation Miracle

~ Brian Gordon ~

3 October 1979

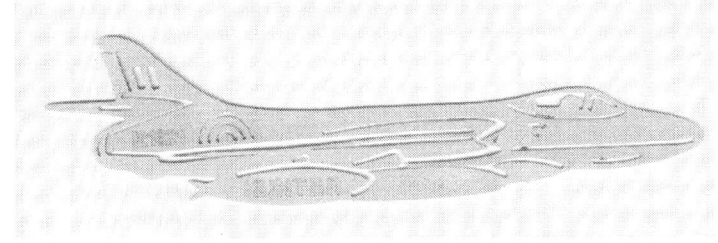

Contents

INTRODUCTION

Tol Janeke

"What is it that makes Op *Miracle* so unique? It was certainly not the first time that the Rhodesian Forces had carried out bold attacks on the enemy, beyond their borders. Nor was it significant in the size of the air or ground effort employed by them. But it was a time when the emphasis was inexorably moving from a bush conflict into a war with sophisticated weapons and technology. The advantage of air superiority, long enjoyed by the Rhodesian Air Force, was slipping away. The crew flying on air operations were well aware that the risks, particularly on cross-border missions, were becoming very high.

Negotiations for a political settlement were underway. Only six short months after Op Miracle, a new government would take over the country. Many Rhodesians had already left their homeland even as it became obvious that the war was drawing to a weary end. The combatants were mentally and physically exhausted and were clamouring for peace.

It was at this time of change that Op Miracle demanded one last, big effort from the Air Force. This was given as always, with courage and determination. These are the qualities that we now seek to honour and remember after all the years. Op Miracle symbolises all that was courageous and audacious in the fighting men and women of Rhodesia. It is a tribute to those that made the ultimate sacrifice."

(Tol Janeke wrote the Introduction to *Rhodesian Air Force Operations with Air Strike Log* – published July 2007. He commanded No 5 Squadron 1971 to 1973 and earned the Jacklin Trophy for the best squadron in the Air Force)

BACKGROUND

Much has been written about the Afro-Rhodesian conflict. Armed aggression continued to escalate, especially with Portugal's withdrawal from Africa. It peaked in the latter half of 1979 – just as the participants to the Lancaster House were gathering in London. Both sides of the armed conflict were pulling out all the stops to gain political leverage at the constitutional talks.

This then is the story about the total loss of a Hawker Hunter fighter ground attack aircraft and a Canberra bomber, both on the same day, the 3rd October 1979. Even more tragically, the loss of the aircrew was the worst experienced by the Air Force in its entire history. When the Black Government came to power, they made no effort to recover the bodies of our fallen colleagues. But, nearly twenty-eight years later former airman Bob Manser miraculously found both the crash sites. The finding was flashed across the globe by the late Eddy Norris and his ORAFs network.

This all happened between July and November 2007. Congratulatory messages flooded in from all over the world – bringing forth mixed emotions. John McKenzie set about making the Operation Miracle Memorial, while Prop Geldenhuys compiled the commemorative booklet. In doing so, the writer has been reduced to tears and fits of anger occasionally. In fact, the writer will be surprised if the same emotions are not experienced by the majority of readers!

As the Op Miracle book went to print, Bob Manser already made plans and found the Donaldson Canberra that was near in the Malvernia.

CHIMOIO CIRCLE

Vila Pery was a popular stop-over for Beira bound Rhodesians. When Portugal handed Moçambique over to FRELIMO (Frente de Libertacão de Moçambique – FPLM) Chimoio, the Vila Pery renamed-town, was garrisoned and the new regime then provided safe haven bases for Zimbabwe ZANLA guerrillas. Rhodesian aerial photography soon identified the various camps that made up the Chimoio Circle, and over thirty hot-pursuit and cross-border strikes were carried out. Two of the more noteworthy operations and strikes are mentioned in this story:

➢ Operation *Dingo* – 23 to 26 November 1977. Casualty numbers were estimated at 800 ZANLA killed and 750 wounded (some sources say it varies from 2000 to 3000). In addition to airman Phil Haigh killed, Trooper GJ Nel was also killed and 6 RLI wounded.

➢ Operation *Miracle* - 21 September to 6 October 1979. This Operation will be remembered for the loss of Brian Gordon and his Hunter and the shooting down of Canberra crews Kevin Peinke and JJ Strydom. The Rhodesian Army lost Gert O'Neill and Ted Mann. (Operation Miracle was the last major cross-border action of the Rhodesian Bush War - Trooper Gert O'Neill was killed on Day 1, clearing trenches. Trooper Mann was tragically killed later, when a captured weapon exploded while being made safe.

➢ Brian carried out a large number of airstrikes on other significant operations like Ops Shovel, Gravel, Vanity, Neutron, Liquid, Racket, Cucumber, Chicory, Carpet, Placid, Oppress, Mascot, Snoopy, Gatling and Uric.

Operation Uric map by Dr JRT Wood – illustrating the Hunter airstrikes in the Gaza Province of Mozambique 1 – 7 September 1979

7

The Chimoio memorial essentially commemorates the Rhodesian Operation *Dingo* air strikes and para-troop assault of 23rd November 1977. It was the biggest attack so far mounted in the war, involving virtually every serviceable aircraft in the Rhodesian Air Force. The huge Chimoio Base complex was situated three hundred and twenty kilometres from New Sarum (Air Force Base), to the north of the town of like name, it housed eight thousand inhabitants, and had become the official headquarters for all the ZANLA forces. Its administrative core was well established with offices, great stores of arms and ammunition, vast stocks of food, a hospital, two schools and several substantial buildings roofed with corrugated iron, and concrete floors. It was a military base heavily defended with 12.7mm and 14.5mm anti-aircraft batteries. War refugees, numbering about twenty thousand at the time, were concentrated at Doeroi, some fifty-five kilometres further east.

Operation *Miracle* followed nearly two years after Operation *Dingo*. However, this time it was a different story altogether (and three Airmen were killed in action, with the loss of an invincible Hunter and a Canberra, all on the same day. The bodies of the downed crews were never recovered. Only the Canberra crash site was 'inspected' very briefly immediately it crashed, but no bodies as such was found. For all intents and purposes, they were "lost" for a very long time).

Air reconnaissance at high level failed to locate any new encampments. Then a Special Air Service force had to be hastily hot-extracted by Alouette helicopter. Next, a two man Selous Scouts call-sign also needed Rhodesian Air Force hot extraction when they ran into armed ZANLA women. The SAS readily admitted that if it had not been for the timely arrival of *The Blues*, the outcome may have been very different – such was the close call. They counted themselves lucky not to have taken casualties. A Canberra then flew another photographic mission over the area and the five camps were identified, facilitating the planning of Operation *Miracle* - which would commence with the Canberra air strike at first light on the ZANLA camp on Day 1.

Canberra bombers initiated the attack on defended strongholds at the commencement of Operation Miracle on 27 September 1979. Kevin Peinke flew in Canberra B2 2519, with his normal navigator, Paul Perioli. They took off at 07h00, dropped 300 x Mark II bombs (Alpha), landing back at base at 08h00

Chimoio memorial at Tembwe, Mozambique

The Chimoio memorial (built by Kevin Tidy) in Moçambique basically commemorates the Rhodesian Air Force's Operation Dingo in 1977

Bob Manser and Kevin Tidy - - Cessna 182 at Chimoio

Bob and Kevin Tidy at Chimoio airfield. Kevin kindly flew Bob around the Operation Miracle area, taking several 'Monte Casino' photographs

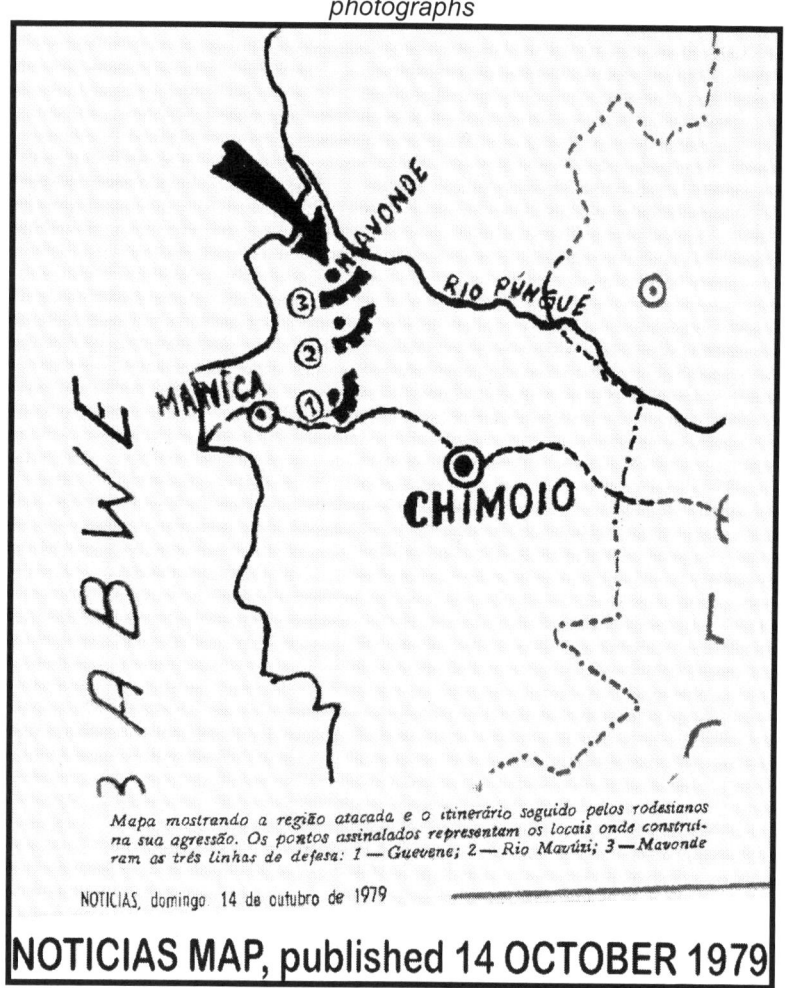

Mapa mostrando a região atacada e o itinerário seguido pelos rodesianos na sua agressão. Os pontos assinalados representam os locais onde construíram as três linhas de defesa: 1 — Guevene; 2 — Rio Mavúzi; 3 — Mavonde

NOTICIAS, domingo 14 de outubro de 1979

NOTICIAS MAP, published 14 OCTOBER 1979

The Maputo Noticias newspaper reported:
"Map showing the attacked region and the itinerary (route) followed by the Rhodesians during their aggression. The arrowed (highlighted) points indicate the areas where they had built their defence lines:
1 – Guevene;
2 – Mavdzi;
3 - Mavonde".

10

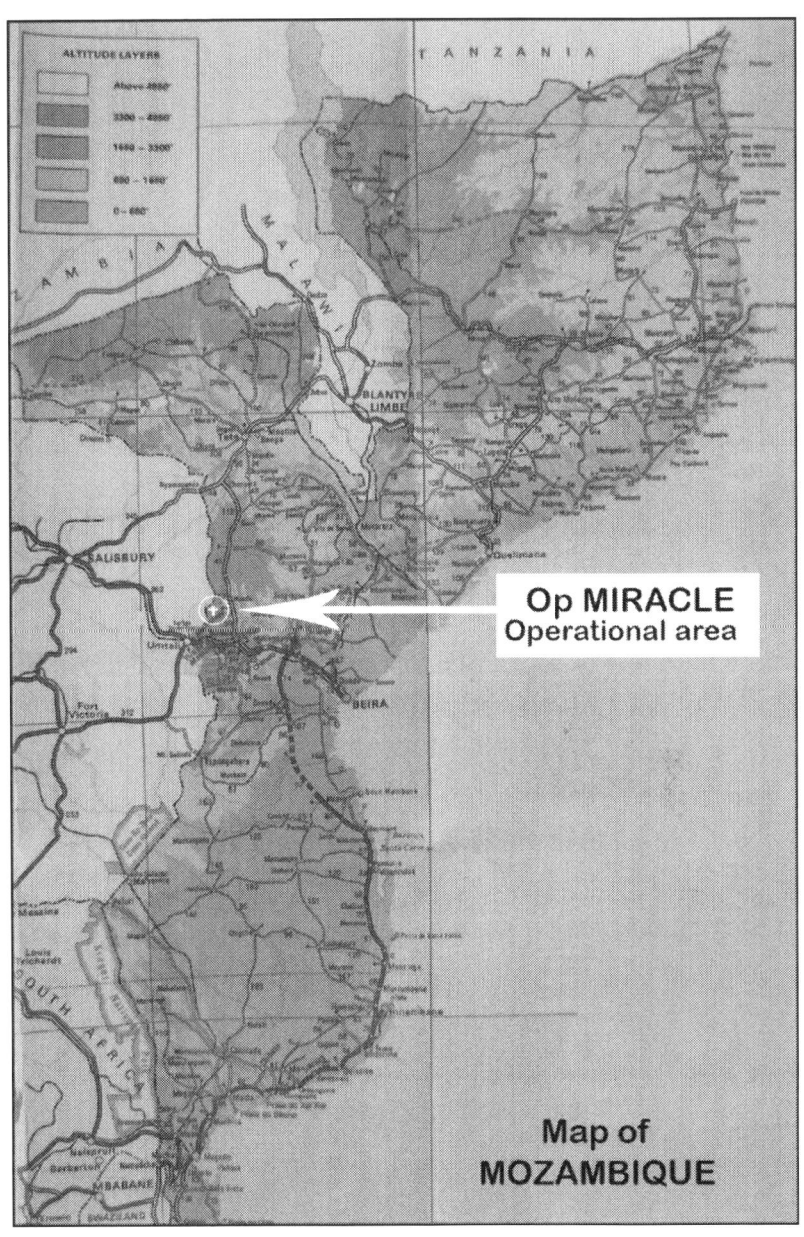

Op MIRACLE
Operational area

Map of
MOZAMBIQUE

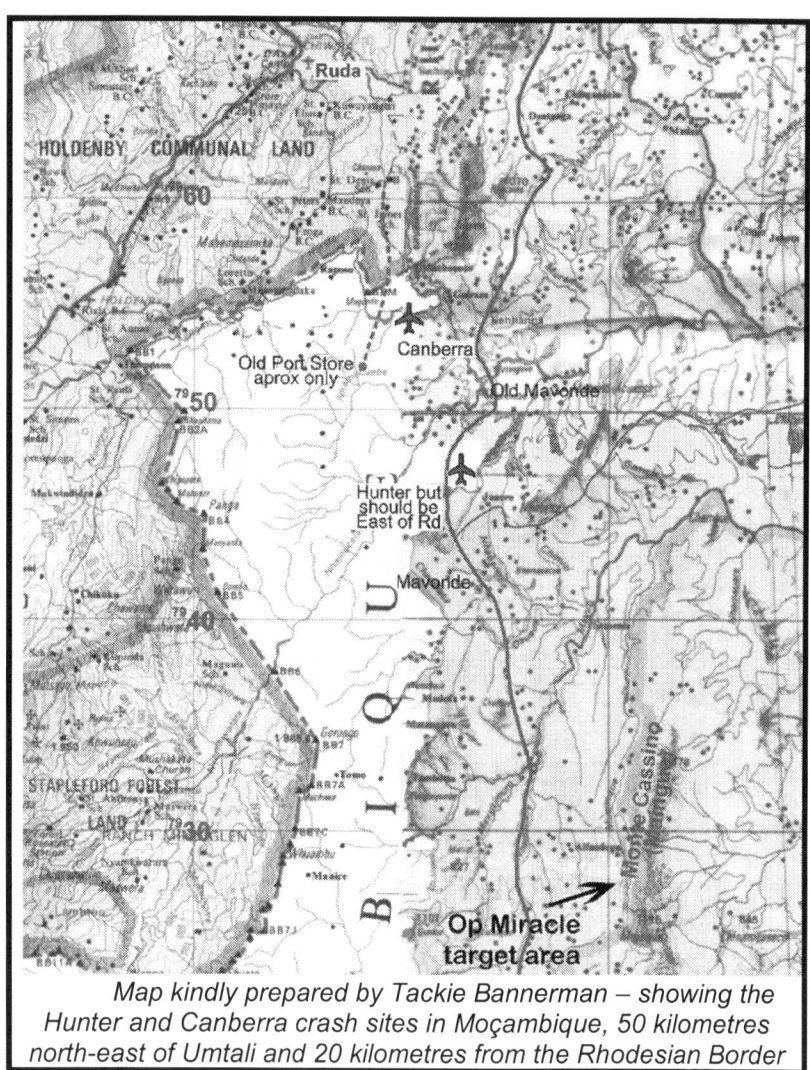

Map kindly prepared by Tackie Bannerman – showing the Hunter and Canberra crash sites in Moçambique, 50 kilometres north-east of Umtali and 20 kilometres from the Rhodesian Border

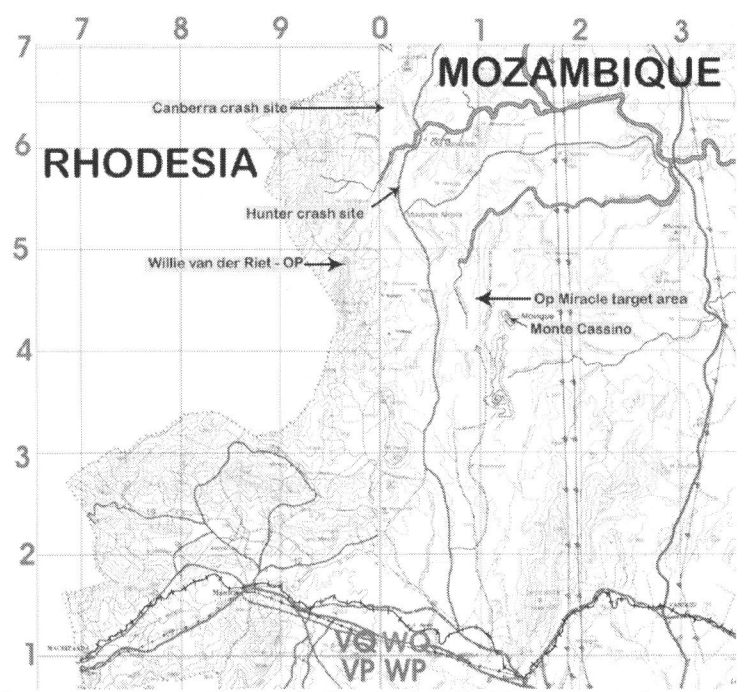

Operation Miracle Map – kindly supplied by Manica historian James "Tackie" Bannerman

13

Evidence of AA Guns – Op Dingo (2 Years earlier)

Maingue / Monte Casino – as first sighted by Bob Manser

MAINGUE – Monte Casino

This photograph of Maingue, dubbed Monte Casino, was taken by Bob Manser in September 2007, while flying with Kevin Tidy in the latter's Cessna 182. Bob is quite at home in the air, having flown Microlights for the past 10 years. Bob and Kevin Tidy were in for a particularly bumpy flight because of several bush-fires, heavy haze, poor visibility and a blustering wind blowing. The photograph shows the terrain that needed neutralisation in order for ComOps to achieve their objective of destroying the well defended Soviet assisted ZANLA base.

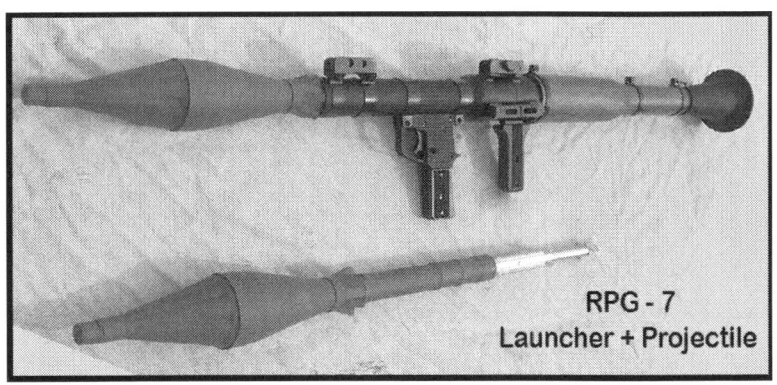

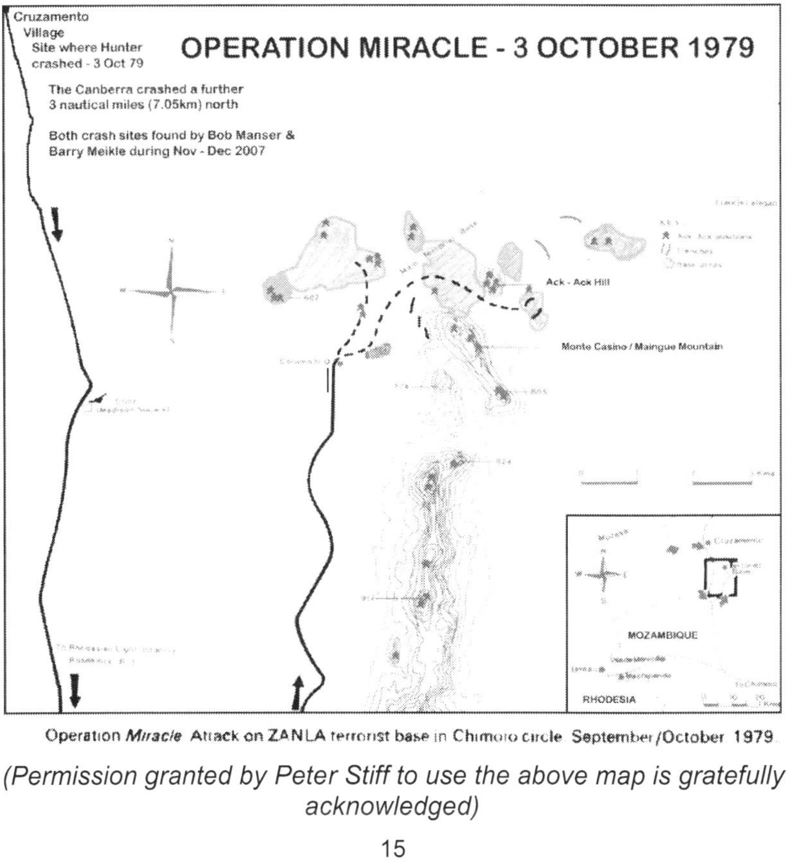

RPG - 7
Launcher + Projectile

OPERATION MIRACLE - 3 OCTOBER 1979
Cruzamento Village
Site where Hunter crashed - 3 Oct 79
The Canberra crashed a further 3 nautical miles (7.05km) north
Both crash sites found by Bob Manser & Barry Meikle during Nov - Dec 2007
Ack - Ack Hill
Monte Casino / Maingue Mountain
MOZAMBIQUE
RHODESIA

Operation *Miracle* Attack on ZANLA terrorist base in Chimoio circle September/October 1979.

(Permission granted by Peter Stiff to use the above map is gratefully acknowledged)

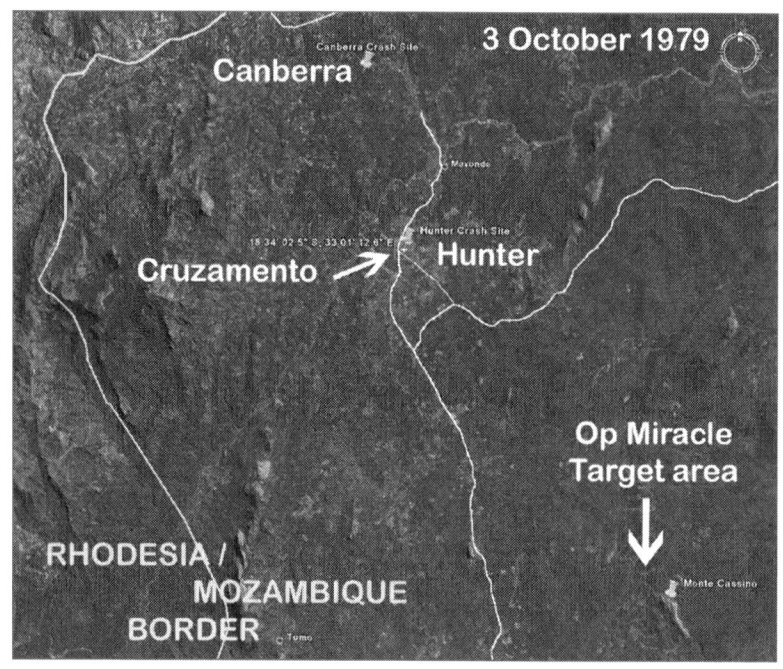

Crash sites in Moçambique

❖ **Hunter**: GPS 18°34'02.5" South 33°01'12.6" East
   - WQ 023473

❖ **Canberra**: GPS 18°30'19.5" South 33°00'16.3" East
   - WQ 008542

Operation Miracle - battle grounds
Hunter and Canberra shot down - 3 October 1979

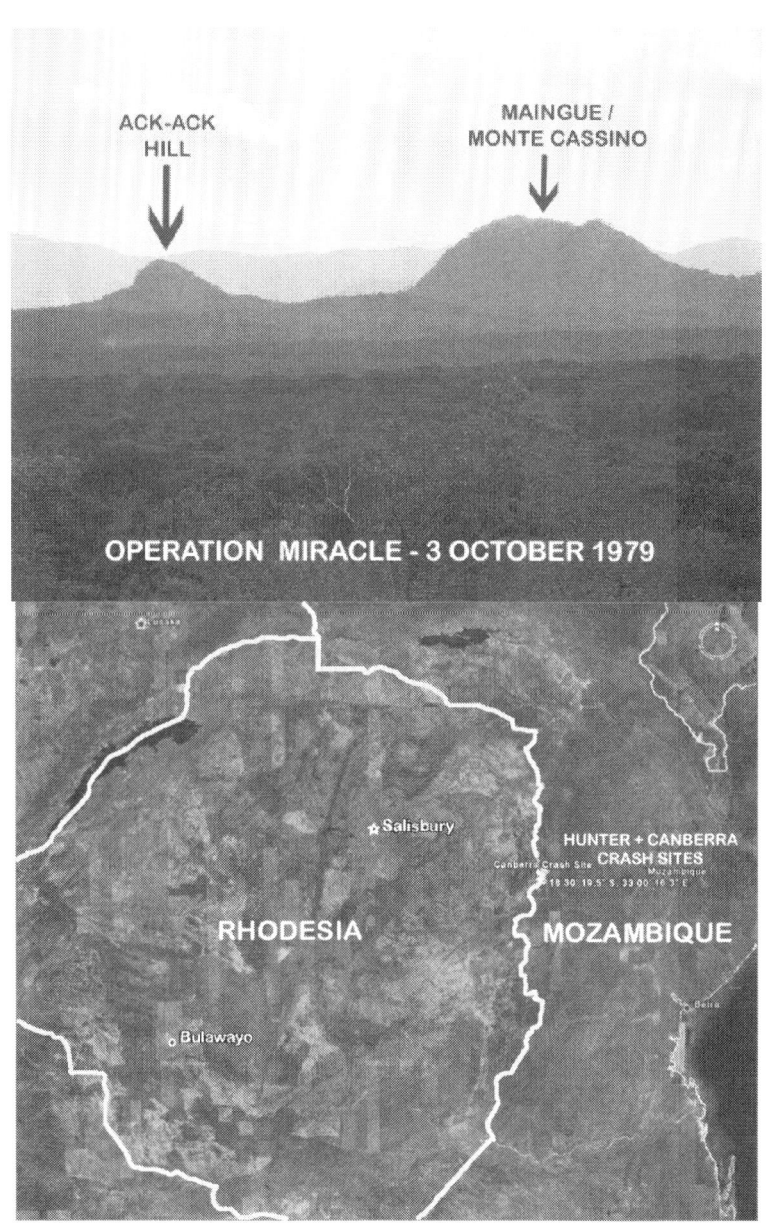

ACK-ACK HILL

MAINGUE / MONTE CASSINO

OPERATION MIRACLE - 3 OCTOBER 1979

Salisbury

HUNTER + CANBERRA CRASH SITES

RHODESIA

MOZAMBIQUE

Bulawayo

Golf Bomb – as displayed in the Tauranga (New Zealand) museum, kindly supplied by Hugh Bomford. No less than 16 of these Petter-Bowyer designed bombs were dropped by the Hunter pilots of No 1 Squadron, on the surrounding strongholds on Maingue / Monte Casino mountain.

OPERATION MIRACLE: 21 SEPTEMBER to 6 OCTOBER 1979

Operation *Miracle* consisted of attacks on five camps which formed the core of the Chimoio Circle - well defended by revetments, linked by trenches and spread over sixty-four square kilometres which could accommodate several thousand inhabitants. Chimoio Circle was Russian-planned and was dominated by a granite kopje dubbed Monte Casino, complete with Russian 12,7mm and 37mm guns.

Prior to the start of Operation *Miracle*, several intelligence-gathering sorties against the Chimoio Circle had been carried out with little success. Possibly the ZANLA High Command had learned their lesson after the complete destruction of the first Chimoio raid in 1976 and Operation *Dingo* in November 1977.

Air Commodore Norman Walsh flying in the Command Dakota, together with Special Air Service Colonel Brian Robinson controlled the operations by day. By night Lieutenant Colonel Ron Reid-Daly would take over. At 07h00 on 3rd October the Canberras went in to attack at low level with bouncing Alpha bombs, against Monte Casino and the nearby gun emplacements. Visibility was poor, largely as a result of the smoke coming out of the bombed areas. Also, at this time of the year, haze was a problem for the aircrews.

Unfortunately, the mobile ground forces column was still seven hours behind schedule and thus the ZANLA forces were able to evacuate their camp. The camp was an incredible 64 square kilometres, far larger than expected. There were so many people there that they had burned fully-grown trees, not merely logs, for their cooking fires. Shoes and clothes lay in heaps as the wearers ran out of them in their haste to escape. Plates of sadza porridge lay scattered in the trenches. When the bomb run had been put in on the camp, the elusive Rex Nhongo (who commanded the Zanla forces) and his driver had jumped into Nhongo's green Land Cruiser and bolted. The driver panicked and crashed into a tree, whereupon the occupants leapt out and ran away. ZANLA commander Josiah Tungamirai, seen hiding in his vehicle under the trees, also managed to get away with his life.

The next day, delayed by adverse weather conditions, the Hunters attacked their targets at 13h00 hours with Golf bombs. The Lynx pilot, flying through an incredibly dense curtain of flak, marked the target for the Hunters.

Hawker Hunter

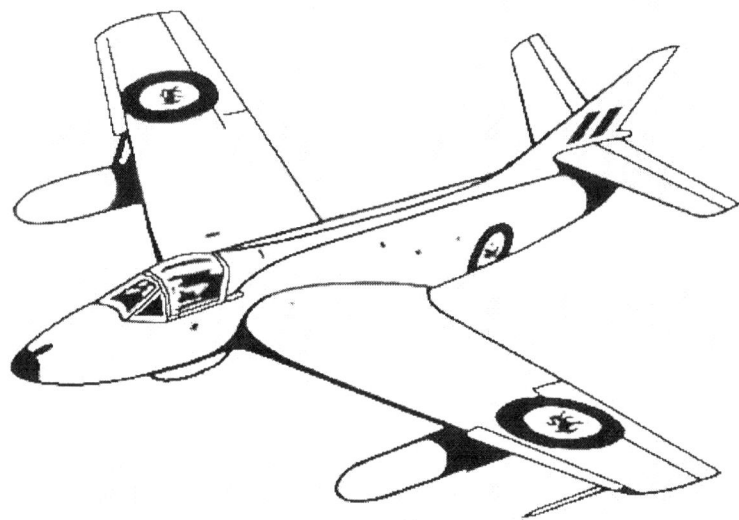

The No 1 Squadron pilots met extremely heavy anti-aircraft fire despite the dropping of sixteen 1000lb Golf bombs striking the defenders and devastating the area. The Hunters were called upon by the ground forces to blast each high point in turn until the high point ridge adjacent to Monte Casino was taken by the Rhodesian troops. Tony Oakley recollects: "The operations around this area were conducted in appalling visibility. My recollection is something more of a ridge line than a gomo away to the right when attacking from south to north. Couldn't help but notice it as it lit up like a firework display any time you came close to it!"

The performance of the aircrews was considered very brave by the Browns (slang for Army personnel), and "...made a deep impression on the troops they were supporting." By now it was dusk. The troops dug in while ZANLA evacuated their strongholds as quickly as they could, leaving for some of the remaining strategic defences.

The following morning the Selous Scouts resumed their attacks, with further help from the Hunters. Monte Casino was reached at about 10h00 hours. The evacuation had been an orderly fighting retreat, and apart from bodies and abandoned equipment, each strongpoint had been held until the right moment.

A sand-bagged anti-aircraft gun-pit - believed found abandoned (but with the gun dis-mantled) by the Scouts on top of Ack-Ack hill, or Monte Casino (Maingue), during the ground assault on Day 3 of Operation Miracle   Picture credit: Keith Samler - according to Peter Stiff

According to the Maputo Noticias newspaper report, it was such a gun that claimed having shot down the Canberra.

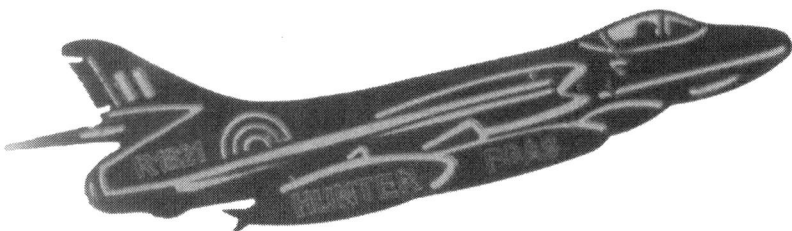

Brian Gordon's Hunter FGA 9 - R1821 - 3 October 1979

The Hunter, and Canberra, in unique stainless-steel cut-outs made especially for the Operation Miracle Memorial. Careful scrutiny will reveal the aircraft numbers – R1821 and R5203 respectively

During the day, Air Lieutenant Brian Gordon in his Hunter FGA 9 was killed whilst carrying out an air strike.

Then the Canberra bombers were called out to neutralise the FRELIMO armoured column. The aircraft were subjected to intense anti-aircraft ground fire. It appears that Air Lieutenant Kevin Peinke made an attack with 50 Alpha bombs and went around for a re-strike. Kevin ran in from south to north, on his first attack, turned around for his second attack, and then appeared to be hit by ground fire. He lost both engines, turned but flew on for only a short distance and then crashed about a kilometre short of the Rhodesian border, near the Girezi River, killing both himself and his navigator, Air Lieutenant J J Strydom.

New updates – email from Eliot Gordon, November 2018

I recently bought the book Rhodesian Air Force Operations with Strike Log with a view of getting a bigger picture of the Operations side of the war and of course the History it contains and finally for a record of Brian's contribution.

We were very disappointed to find our son Brian is hardly mentioned in the Strike Log only Twice and his Death. As I have his Flying Log Book, I have copied the Strike Log format only for the Hunter strikes and included his contribution to the strikes that took place and his contribution was a considerable 74 Strikes in 15 months.

For a young pilot having gone from Wings to 1 Squadron I feel this is a massive achievement. The Object of this exercise is to recognize his contribution and correct history which as it stands at the moment is not representative of who was involved.

This Matter is very close to our Hearts and we hope it can be corrected. the Updated file is on an Excel sheet attached. (Authors note: reproduced later on).

Operation Miracle – Original eBook

This tragic event which, when added to our other losses, meant the Rhodesian Air Force had suffered its worst losses in any operation of the war. The kill ratio was small in relation to the immense effort entailed. When Monte Casino was eventually taken, a grand total of eleven enemy bodies were located. It was assumed the enemy had carried a lot of their dead and wounded away with them. Approximately two thousand out of a possible twelve thousand had defended Chimoio Circle. The protracted operation had permitted most of the enemy to take the gap in haste. History will show that ZANLA was given early warning (betrayal by the British. This accounts for the low casualty rate, since the element of surprise was lost by the attacking forces) and abandoned huge quantities of military and logistic equipment such as the Russian 12,7mm and 37mm guns, food, medical supplies, documents and records.

Also captured were John and Janet, the two tame air raid warning baboons, which became excited and noisy whenever an aircraft approached even at a distance.

During the night FRELIMO mounted an attack using six Soviet T-34 tanks and infantry. But they quickly withdrew after sustaining a direct hit from a Rhodesian Artillery twenty-five pounder shell. The next morning No 4 Squadron Lynxes spotted the tanks but before an air strike could be mounted the tanks had vanished.

The next day, the Rhodesians withdrew their forces nineteen kilometres back across the border.

25-pdr Rhodesian Artillery – scoring a direct hit on a Russian T-34 Tank supplied to Frelimo forces

23

HUNTER AIRSTRIKES 30 JULY 1978 TO 03 OCTOBER 1979

No	Date	Aircrew	Target	Aircraft
846	30/07/1978 Mascot (External)	Vic Wightman J R Blythe-Wood Tony Oakley Varky Varkevisser Steve Kesby Brian Gordon	Tembue 2 Op Mascot	Hunter 1817 Hunter 1198 Hunter 8122 Vamp 1378 Vampire Vamp FB9 812
848	31/07/1978	J R Blythe-Wood Tony Oakley Brian Gordon	Top Cover Op Mascot	Hunter 8116 Hunter 1258 Vamp 8128
1117	2/8/1978	Tony Oakley Brian Gordon	A/T 03/01	Hunter 1198 Vamp 1835
858	01/09/1978	Vic Wightman J R Blythe-Wood Brian Gordon	Op Snoopy Fire Force trooping	Hunter 8116 Hunter 1817 Hunter 1198
	18/09/78	Brian Gordon	Top Cover	Hunter 1817
868	20/09/78	Vic Wightman Alf Wild J R Blythe-Wood Tony Oakley Dave Bourhill Brian Gordon Varky Varkevisse	Op Snoopy Supress AA - A/T 1343. Attack 25 camps, spread over 33kms	Hunter 8112 Hunter Hunter 1821 Hunter 1817 Hunter Hunter 8116 Vamp1380
869	20/09/78	J R Blythe-Wood Tony Oakley Brian Gordon	Op Snoopy A/T 1343	Hunter 1827 Hunter 1158 Hunter 8116
870	21/09/78	Vic Wightman J R Blythe-Wood Tony Oakley Brian Gordon Varky Varkevisse	Op Snoopy Destroyed 3 armoured personnel carriers	Hunter 1827 Hunter 1822 Hunter 1286 Hunter 8116 Vamp 1380
871	21/09/78	Vic Wightman J R Blythe-Wood Tony Oakley Brian Gordon Brian Gordon Varky Varkevisser Steve Kesby	Op Snoopy A/T 1343 - See above Chimoio circle	Hunter 8116 Hunter 1286 Hunter 1817 Hunter 8122 Hunter 1198 Vamp 1380 Vampire

No	Date	Aircrew	Target	Aircraft
886	18/10/78	J R Blythe-Wood Tony Oakley Brian Gordon	A/T 1509 Frans	Hunter 1286 Hunter 8122 Hunter 1188
887	19/10/78 Op Gatling	Tony Oakley J R Blythe-Wood Dave Bourhill Alf Wild Jim Stagman Brian Gordon Cocky Beneke Tol Janeke	ZIPRA Chikumbi camp and Westlands Farm (Green Leaders fame) A/T 1521	Hunter 8122 Hunter 1286 Hunter Hunter Hunter Hunter 1188 Vamp 8129 Vamp1378
889	20/10/78	J R Blythe-Wood Brian Gordon	Op Gatling Top cover	Hunter 1188 Hunter 1827
890	21/10/78	J R Blythe-Wood Tony Oakley Brian Gordon	Top cover Brian x 3 sorties	Hunter 1827 Hunter 1821 Hunter 8116
	02/11/78	Brian Gordon	UC - Frans	Hunter 1286
896	05/11'78	Vic Wightman Brian Gordon	A/T 05 (Op Jacket)	Hunter 8116 Hunter 1827
900	17/11/78	Vic Wightman Brian Gordon	A/T 1682 Mtoko	Hunter 1827 Hunter 8116
904	29/11/78	Vic Wightman Tony Oakley Brian Gordon	Munitions hanger at Tete	Hunter 1286 Hunter 1827 Hunter 1286
908	08/12/78	Vic Wightman Ginger Baldwin Jim Stagman Tony Oakley Dave Bourhill Brian Gordon	Moatize Hangar, near Tete, plus ZANLA Tete barrack block	Hunter 8116 Hunter Hunter Hunter 1817 Hunter Hunter 1286
909	09/12/78	Vic Wightman Tony Oakley Brian Gordon	30mm 68RP 68RP	Hunter 1821 Hunter 1827 Hunter 1286
910	20/12/78	Vic Wightman Jim Stagman Ginger Baldwin Brian Gordon	6 x ZANLA vehicles a petrol bowser Chimoio to Tete	Hunter 1827 Hunter Hunter Hunter 8122

No	Date	Aircrew	Target	Aircraft
911	22/12/78	Vic Wightman Varky Varkevisser Steve Kesby? Brian Gordon	Mboroma - ZIPRA Terr camp 140kms N of Border	Hunter 1821 Vamp 1378 Vampire Hunter 1821
913	24/12/78	Vic Wightman Brian Gordon Brian Gordon	A/T 1914 & A/T 1919 - Nails	Hunter 1821 Hunter 1817 Hunter 1821
915	27/12/78	Vic Wightman Tony Oakley Brian Gordon	A/T 1937 30mm and 1000lb	Hunter 1821 Hunter Hunter 8116
919	29/12/78	Vic Wightman Tony Oakley Brian Gordon	Comops task 30 mm and 68RP	Hunter 1284 Hunter 8116 Hunter 1827
920	30/12/78	Vic Wightman Brian Gordon	A/T	Hunter 1284 Hunter 8116
922	01/01/79	Vic Wightman Tony Oakley Brian Gordon	A/T 007 30 mm & 68RP	Hunter 1821 Hunter 1188 Hunter 1284
928	07/01/79	Vic Wightman Tony Oakley Brian Gordon	Supply truck, N of Tembue VU8270 Moz	Hunter 1284 Hunter 1817 Hunter 1827
929	09/01/79	Brian Gordon		Hunter 1817
	30/01/79	Brian Gordon		
953	23/02/79	Vic Wightman Brian Gordon	2 Zipra camps W of Lusaka	Hunter 1188 Hunter 1286
956	01/03/79	Vic Wightman Brian Gordon	Zanla bldgs. at Mutarara Tete	Hunter 1284 Hunter 8116
959	12/03/79	Vic Wightman Brian Gordon	Chokwe Zanla HQ	Hunter 1284 Hunter 8116
961	14/03/79	Vic Wightman	Tete airfield	Hunter
962	16/03/79	Vic Wightman Tony Oakley Brian Gordon	ZANLA arms dump at Dondo Moz	Hunter 1188 Hunter 1284 Hunter 8116
963	17/03/1979 Neutron (External)	Vic Wightman Tony Oakley Brian Gordon	Vanduzi, Chimoio town Moz A/T 459	Hunter 1188 Hunter 8116 Hunter 1284
	26/03/79	Tony Oakley	A/T	Tony Oakley

No	Date	Aircrew	Target	Aircraft
972	10/4/1979 Liquid (External)	Vic Wightman Varky Varkevisser Tony Oakley Brian Gordon	Zambia A/T 651 & 652 A/T 651 & A/T 642	Hunter 1198 Hunter 1286 Hunter 8116 Hunter 1258
973	11/04/79	Vic Wightman Varky Varkevisse Tony Oakley Brian Gordon	Mulungushi - Operation Liquid	Hunter 1198 Hunter 1286 Hunter 8116 Hunter 1258
975	12/04/79	Vic Wightman Tony Oakley Brian Gordon	Op Racket - Top LH cnr of Zambia	Hunter 1284 Hunter 8116 Hunter 1258
977	14/04/79	Hunter 1284 Hunter 8116 Hunter 1258	Mulungushi - Zambia ZIPRA camp.	Hunter 1198 Hunter 1284 Hunter 1258
979	20/04/79	Vic Wightman Tony Oakley Brian Gordon	Air Task - unknown	Hunter 1198 Hunter 1286 Hunter 1258
980	21/04/79	Vic Wightman Tony Oakley Brian Gordon	Op Grapple Air Task	Hunter 1198 Hunter 1188 Hunter 1284
981	22/04/79	Vic Wightman Brian Gordon	30mm, 68mm 68RP	Hunter 1198 Hunter 1284
983	26/04/79	Vic Wightman Tony Oakley Varky Varkevisser Brian Gordon	Op Grapple Air Task	Hunter 1198 Hunter 1188 Hunter 1829 Hunter 1284
985	29/04/79	Vic Wightman Tony Oakley	Operation Oppress	Hunter 1258 Hunter 1188
988	07/05/79 Thrasher	Vic Wightman Ginger Baldwin	Op Burma Valley VP	Hunter 1198 Hunter
989	11/05/79	Tony Oakley Brian Gordon	A/T u/k – Golf bombs	Hunter 1286 Hunter 1188
990	12/05/79	Tony Oakley	VP841612	Hunter 1188
991	13/05/79	Vic Wightman Tony Oakley Brian Gordon	30mm, 68mm RP, Golf Bombs	Hunter 1188 Hunter 1826 Hunter 1258
992	15/05/79	Tony Oakley Brian Gordon	68mm Matra 68mm RP	Hunter 1284 Hunter 1198

No	Date	Aircrew	Target	Aircraft
998	04/06/79 External	Vic Wightman Tony Oakley Brian Gordon	Chivinga Tete Prov Moz	Hunter 8116 Hunter Hunter 1258
1000	08/06/79	Tony Oakley Brian Gordon	A/T 1304 - Op Tangent	Hunter 1198 Hunter 1284
1135	08/06/79	Tony Oakley Brian Gordon	A/T 1319	Hunter 1198 Hunter 8116
1003	22/06/79	Vic Wightman Brian Gordon	A/T 1392	Hunter 1188 Hunter 1284
1004	26/06/79 Carpet External	Vic Wightman Tony Oakley Brian Gordon	ZIPRA camp at Chikumbi N of Lusaka	Hunter 8116 Hunter 1188 Hunter 1198
1006	01/07/79 Chicory External	Vic Wightman Varky Varkevisse Tony Oakley Brian Gordon	Munitions and supply depot. 35kms W of Lusaka	Hunter 8116 Hunter 8122 Hunter 1188 Hunter 1821
1008	07/07/79 Fiddle	Vic Wightman Varky Varkevisse Tony Oakley Brian Gordon	Op Fiddle. Fire Force Zimbabwe Ruins	Hunter 1827 Hunter 1284 Hunter 8116 Hunter 1258
1009	8/7/1979 Cucumber External	Vic Wightman Tony Oakley Brian Gordon	LL attack. Cabora Bassa Mozambique	Hunter 1827 Hunter 1198 Hunter 1284
1011	20/07/79 External	Vic Wightman Tony Oakley Brian Gordon	Cindy Plots. ZIPRA base nr Livingston	Hunter 1258 Hunter 1198 Hunter 1188
1026	22/08/79 External	Vic Wightman Tony Oakley Brian Gordon	6 tgts known as Moscow in Zambia	Hunter 1284 Hunter 1198 Hunter 1286
1027	22/08/179 Op Placid	Vic Wightman Tony Oakley Brian Gordon	Zambia Golf bombs	Hunter 1286 Hunter 1198 Hunter 1284
1029	23/08/79 Placid External	Vic Wightman Tony Oakley Ziggy Seegmuller Brian Gordon	Rafunsa and Solwezi (Qumbo's Base)	Hunter 1284 Hunter 1827 Hunter Hunter 1286

No	Date	Aircrew	Target	Aircraft
1032	02/09/79 Uric External	Varky Varkevisse Tony Oakley Ziggy Seegmuller Brian Gordon	Moz bridges, Conbomune, Mabalane, Barragem	Hunter 1198 Hunter 1816 Hunter 8 Hunter 1258
1035	05/09/79 Uric External	Vic Wightman Varky Varkevisser Tony Oakley Ziggy Seegmuller Guy Dixon Brian Gordon	As above – Alex Weston KIA – Bell shot down Barragem	Hunter 1284 Hunter 1188 Hunter 1258 Hunter Hunter Hunter 1286
1036	05/09/79 Uric External	Vic Wightman Varky Varkevisse Tony Oakley Ziggy Seegmuller Brian Gordon	As above -	Hunter 1284 Hunter 1188 Hunter 1258 Hunter Hunter 1286
1037	06/09/79 Uric External	Vic Wightman Varky Varkevisse Tony Oakley Ziggy Seegmuller Guy Dixon Brian Gordon	As Above – Puma shot down – A/T 1835 -1837	Hunter 1284 Hunter 1188 Hunter 1821 Hunter Hunter Hunter 1286
1038	07/09/79 Uric External	Vic Wightman Tony Oakley Ziggy Seegmuller Guy Dixon Brian Gordon	Uric (External) Air Task 1837	Hunter 1284 Hunter 1198 Hunter Hunter Hunter 1286
1039	12/09/79	Vic Wightman Brian Gordon	A/T 1838	Hunter 1821 Hunter 1817
1040	13/09/79	Varky Varkevisse Brian Gordon	A/T 1926	Hunter 1298 Hunter 1284
1050	15/09/79	Brian Gordon	Monte Xilvuo relay station	Hunter 1198
1044	24/09/79	Tony Oakley Brian Gordon	A/T 1938	Hunter 1284 Hunter 1817

No	Date	Aircrew	Target	Aircraft
1046	27/09/79 Operation Miracle	Kevin Peinke / Paul Perioli V. Wightman JR Blythe-Wood John Annan Ziggy Seegmuller Brian Gordon Brian Gordon (2nd) Brian Gordon (3rd)	Monte Casino, Moçambique Golf Bombs, 30mm, 68mm RP 30mm, 68mm RP A/T 1974 - 76	Canberra 2519 Hunter Hunter Hunter Hunter Hunter 1258 Hunter 1821 Hunter 1198
1051		Vic Wightman Ziggy Seegmuller Brian Gordon Brian Gordon Brian Gordon		
1051	28/09/79 Miracle	Kevin Peinke / Paul Perioli Mike Huson G-Car V. Wightman Ziggy Seegmuller Brian Gordon Brian-2nd and 3rd)	Monte Casino, New Chimoio Hill 761	Canberra 2055 Lynx G-Car x 12 Hunter Hunter Hunter
1052	29/09/79 Miracle	Vic Wightman Kevin Peinke / Paul Perioli Vic Wightman Ziggy Seegmuller Kevin Peinke / Paul Perioli	Monte Casino	Hunter Canberra 2519 Hunter Hunter Canberra 2519
1054	03/10/79 Miracle	Baldy Baldwin JR Blythe-Wood Guy Dixon Brian Gordon Ziggy Seegmuller Tony Oakley Varky Varkevisser	Chimoio — convoy of vehicles at Cruzamento cross-roads Air Task 2046 WQ 023473	Hunter Hunter Hunter Hunter Hunter Hunter Hunter

No	Date	Aircrew	Target	Aircraft
1055	03/10/79 Operation Miracle	Mike Huson Dave Rowe / Paul Perioli Kevin Peinke / JJ Strydom John Annan Ziggy Seegmuller	Chimoio – Neutralise Armoured column – Grid Reference WQ 008542	Lynx Canberra 2055 Canberra 5203 Hunter Hunter

Excel prepared by Elliot Gordon of Brian's Log Book vs Rhodesian Airstrike Logs is reproduced below. The author has inserted brief write-ups of the more significant airstrikes that Brian Gordon carried out.

NUMBER; DATE-OP AREA; AIRCREW; TARGET; AIRCRAFT; WEAPONS EXPENDED; RESULT

845   28/07/1978; J R Blythe-Wood; 982; SAS Air Task 982; Hunter 1258 Tony Oakley Hunter 1816;

846   30/07/1978 Mascot (External); Vic Wightman; Tembue 2; Hunter 1817; 30mm cannon, Matra; Melon. Hunters and Canberras returned, J R Blythe-Wood; Hunter 1198 Frantan and Golf after re-arming. Tony Oakley Hunter 8122 Bombs; Tony confirms three airstrikes/re-strikes carried out. Varky Varkevisser Vampire 1378 See also Winds of Destruction Pg 491 Steve Kesby; Vampire; Brian Gordon; Op Mascot; Vampire FB9 8128

848   31/07/1978 J R Blythe-Wood Top Cover; Hunter 8116; Two top cover sorties; Tony Oakley; Hunter 1258; Brian Gordon; Op Mascot, Vampire FB9 8128; Top Cover

Operation _Mascot_: - 10 July to 1August 1978 was a ground and air assault on the Tembue base north of Cabora Bassa Dam believed to accommodate about five hundred terrorists. Eight Dakotas was used to drop 128 SAS and RLI paras to surround the target but most of the inhabitants managed to escape to the west before ground contact was made.

1117   2/8/1978; Tony Oakley; Hunter 1198; Brian Gordon; A/T 03/01; Vampire FB9 1835

858   01/09/1978 – Snoopy; Vic Wightman; Fire Force trooping and; Hunter 8116; 20mm cannon; JR two sorties; J R Blythe-Wood; top cover. SAS Op Snoopy; Hunter 1817; Brian Gordon; A/T 1224 Blue; Hunter 1198; Two sorties
18/09/1978; Brian Gordon; A/T 1323; Hunter 1817; Top Cover

868 20/09/1978 - Snoopy (External); Vic Wightman; Supress AA, Attack 25 camps, spread - A/T 1343: Hunter 8112; Golf bombs; SAS trooper Steve Donnelly KIA, accidently killed by Golf Bomb; Alf Wild; Hunter; Dave ; J R Blythe-Wood; over 33kms² - Chimoio Hunter 1821; and Glen both hit by Strela - Dave below; Tony Oakley; Circle, approx. 70; Hunter 1817; starboard aileron, and Canberra port; Dave Bourhill; from the Rhodesian border; Hunter; engine; Brian Gordon; A/T 1343; Hunter 8116; Fran, 68mm; 3 Sorties; Varky Varkevisser; Vampire 1380; See Winds of Destruction Pg 497

869 20/09/1978 - Snoopy (External); J R Blythe-Wood; A/T 1343; Hunter 1827; Aircraft change - See above; Tony Oakley; Hunter 1158; Brian Gordon; Hunter 8116; Fran, 68mm; 3 Sorties

870 21/09/1978 - Snoopy (External); Vic Wightman; Destroyed three armoured personnel carriers; Hunter 1827; 20mm cannon + RP's; Destroyed; J R Blythe-Wood; Hunter 1822; Hunters two op sorties; Tony Oakley; Hunter 1286; JR x 3 sorties; Brian Gordon; A/T 1343; Hunter 8116; Fran, 68 mm; 3 Sorties; Varky Varkevisser; Vampire 1380.

871 22/09/1978; Vic Wightman; A/T 1343 - See above, Chimoio Circle; Hunter 8116; 300mm cannon; Hunters two op sorties; J R Blythe-Wood; Hunter 1286; 68RP; Tony Oakley; Hunter 1817; Brian Gordon; A/T 1343; Hunter 8122; 2 Sorties ;Brian Gordon; Hunter 1198; Varky Varkevisser; Vampire 1380; Steve Kesby; Vampire.

Operation *Snoopy* was another major external operation mounted by the SAS and RLI against 25 Zanla camps within the Chimoio Circle – some 70km east from the Rhodesian/Mozambique border. The target was ten times bigger than originally thought, being some thirty kilometres by forty kilometres and consisting of small camps. The haze that hung over the targets worsened once the camps began burning. The Hunters destroyed three Russian armoured personnel carriers that arrived in the camp. The Herald headline of September 25 read: "Border Raids: 25 Camps hit. Mission success: Frelimo forces among dead".

886 18/10/1978; J R Blythe-Wood; A/T 1509; Hunter 1286; Tony Oakley; Hunter 8122; Brian Gordon; A/T 1509; Hunter 1188; Frans

887 19/10/1978 – Op Gatling (External); Tony Oakley; ZIPRA Chikumbi camp and Westlands Farm (Green Leaders fame); Hunter 8122; Golf Bombs and Frans; J R Blythe-Wood; Hunter 1286; Dave Bourhill; A/T 1521; Hunter; ; Alf Wild; Hunter; Jim Stagman; Hunter; Brian Gordon; Hunter 1188; 1 Golf, 1 x 1000

pound and 30mm; Cocky Beneke; Vampire 8129; Tol Janeke; Vampire 1378

889 20/10/1978 - Gatling (External); J R Blythe-Wood; CGT - 2 Camps 100kms; Hunter 1286; Total casualties for the 3 ops were 396 SE of Lusaka killed, 719 wounded and 192 missing; Refer Winds of Destruction Pg 503; Brian Gordon; A/T 1521; Hunter 1188; Top Cover 2 Sorties; Brian Gordon; Hunter 1827; Top Cover

890 21/10/1978 - Gatling (External); J R Blythe-Wood; A/T 1521 - as above; Hunter 1286; JR x 2 sorties, second in Hunter 1827; Tony Oakley; Hunter 8122; Brian Gordon; Hunter 1827; Top Cover; 3 Sorties; Hunter 1821; Fran 30mm; Hunter 8116; Top Cover 2/11/1978; Brian Gordon; UC; Hunter 1286; Fran.

Operation *Gatling*: - Gatling was preceded with a diversionary attack on Zanla encampments along the Pungwe River in Mozambique before mounting the attack on Westlands Farm near Lusaka, Zambia at 08h30 on 19th October 1978. This attack was popularized by John Edmonds' ballad 'Green Leader'.

896 05/11/1978 - Op Jacket (External); Vic Wightman; Hunter 8116; Pride of Eagles Pg 637; Brian Gordon; A/T 05; Hunter 1827; Fran

900 17/11/1978; Vic Wightman; A/T 1680; Hunter 1827; 30mm 68RP; Brian Gordon; A/T 1682 (Matoko); Hunter 8116; Fran and 30mm

904 29/11/1978 - Op Shovel (External); Vic Wightman; Main munitions hanger at Tete; Hunter 1821; 30mm cannon 68RP; Single rocket caused colossal explosion.; Hunter 1817; SAS destroyed nearby railway bridge; Tony Oakley; Hunter 1286; Brian Gordon A/T 1761; Hunter 1827; 1000-pound bombs.; 2 Sorties; Brian Gordon; Hunter 1286

908 08/12/1978 (External); Vic Wightman; Moatize Hangar, near Tete, plus ZANLA Tewte barrack block Hunter 8116; 4 x Golf bombs, 30mm cannon and 68RP; Ammunitions, arsenal destroyed, barrack block flattened as per PB's Winds of Destruction Page506; Ginger Baldwin; Hunter; Jim Stagman; Hunter; Tony Oakley; Hunter 1817; Dave Bourhill; Hunter; Brian Gordon; Hunter 1286; Golf , 30mm 68RP; One Golf bomb hung up.

909 9/12/1978; Vic Wightman; Hunter 1821; 30mm 68RP; Tony Oakley; Hunter 1827; Brian Gordon; Hunter 1286; 68RP.

Operation *Shovel*: - An earlier capture revealed that a Tete airfield hangar contained a large supply of arms and explosives – and that the resupply for Tete was by rail, from Beira to Moatize which was the nearest railway siding to Tete. The SAS was tasked to blow the bridge while No 1 Squadron was tasked to air strike the airfield hangar. The leader's rockets fell short but the number two made no mistake with his rockets scored a direct hit. The massive arms dump (3,000 land mines) hoarded in the hangar blasted the hangar itself, plus the surrounding buildings off the face of the earth. The SAS were equally successful with their task and waited for a steam train to appear – destined to end its journey at the bottom of the Zambezi river bed.

910 20/12/1978; Vic Wightman; ZANLA convoy of six vehicles, including a petrol bowser off the Chimoio to Tete road; Hunter 1827; Jim Stagman; Hunter; Ginger Baldwin; Hunter; Brian Gordon; A/T 1899; Hunter 8122; 30mm canon

911 22/12/1978; Vic Wightman; Mboroma - ZIPRA Terr Hunter 1821; Rescue of 100 prisoners camp 140kms North of Border; Varky Varkevisser; Vampire 1378; Steve Kesby; Vampire; Brian Gordon; Hunter 1821; Top cover; Pride of Eagles Page 643. 18 enemy killed

913 24/12/1978; Vic Wightman; Hunter 1821; 30mm 68RP; Two Sorties 2nd in Hunter 8116; Brian Gordon A/T 1914; Hunter 1817; Nails; Two sorties; Brian Gordon; A/T 1919; Hunter 1821; Nails

915 27/12/1978; Vic Wightman; A/T 1937; Hunter 1821; 30mm 68RP; Two op sorties; Tony Oakley; Hunter; Brian Gordon; Hunter 8116; 1000 lb and 30mm

919 29/12/1978; Vic Wightman; Comops Task; Hunter 1284; 30mm 68RP; Tony Oakley; Hunter 8116; Golf bombs; Brian Gordon; Hunter 1827; 30mm 68RP

920 30/12/1978; Vic Wightman; Hunter 1284; 30mm 68RP; Brian Gordon; Hunter 8116

922 1/1/1979 Vic Wightman; Comops Task; Hunter 1821; 30mm 68RP; Tony Oakley; Hunter 1188; Brian Gordon; A/T 007; Hunter 1284; Top Cover

928 7/1/1979 ; Vic Wightman; Supply truck, North of Tembue - VU 8270, Mozambique; Hunter 1284 30mm canon; Tony Oakley; Hunter 1817; Golf bombs, Brian Gordon; A/T 179; Hunter 1827

929 9/1/1979; Brian Gordon; Hot extraction; Hunter 1817; Terr RPK gunner killed. See JRT Wood - Page 297
30/1/1979; Brian Gordon, A/T 179; Hunter 1286; 2 x Golf bombs

953 23/02/1979; Vic Wightman; Two ZIPRA camps, West of Lusaka; Hunter 1188; 2 Sorties; Brian Gordon; Hunter 1286; 2 Sorties.

Operation _Grovel_: - This was a Canberra and Hunter air strike on two Zipra camps west of Lusaka in Zambia, resulting in the death of 18 and wounding of 114 enemy.

Operation _Vanity_;- This was the air strike of the Zipra base at Luso in Angola – 1000km from the Rhodesian border, in retaliation for the downing of the second Viscount _Umniati_ – in which all 59 people on board were killed.

956   1/3/1979; Vic Wightman; ZANLA buildings at Mutarara, (External) in the Tete province of Mozambique; Hunter 1284; 30mm canon ; JRT Wood Page 324. Zambians claimed on; 3 March that the air raid killed five women and injured two; GR YR5070; Brian Gordon   A/T 334; Hunter 8116; 68RP

959   12/3/1979; Vic Wightman; Arms depot at Chokwe and a ZANLA; Hunter 1284; Brian Gordon   A/T 425; Hunter 8116; 68RP; Sixteen ZANLA killed and 7 injured HQ and barracks at Barragem in the Gaza province of Mozambique

961   14/03/1979; Vic Wightman; Tete Airfield; Hunter 1284; 30mm canon; Tete airfield as per Vic.

962   16/03/1979; Vic Wightman; ZANLA arms, ammunition explosives dump at Dondo, North of Beira, Mozambique and ;Hunter 1188; 30mm canon; JRT Wood Page 325 Air Task 457 - as per Tony Oakley; Hunter 1284; Oakley Log book input - 68mm Matra; Brian Gordon A/T 457; Hunter 8116; 68RP

963   17/03/1979; Op Neutron; Vic Wightman; Vanduzi, 15kms from Chimoio town, Mozambique Manica Province, SAS and 1RLI.; (External); Air Task 459; Hunter 1188; 30mm cannon; JRT Wood and Pride of Eagles Page 650.;Tony Oakley; Hunter 8116; 68mm RP; Golf bombs; Peter Bowyer - Winds of Destruction; Brian GordonA/T 459; Hunter 1284; Golf bombs 26/03/1979; Tony Oakley; Hunter 1284

972   10/4/1979; SAS and 1RLI.; (External – Op Liquid); SAS and 1RLI; Air Task 459; Vic Wightman; Zambia A/T 651 & 652; Hunter 1198; Golf bombs; Ex Vic Falls; Varky Varkevisser; Hunter 1286; Air Task 459; Tony Oakley; Hunter 8116; Brian Gordon; A/T 651 & A/T 642; Hunter 1258; Golf bomb & 30mm - Two sorties

973   11/4/1979; Vic Wightman; Mulungushi - Operation Liquid; Hunter 1198; 6 x 1000lbs; PB,s Winds of Destruction - Page 522/523; Varky Varkevisser; Hunter 1286; 30mm cannon; Tony Oakley; Hunter 8116; 68mm RP; Brian Gordon; Hunter 1258; Golf Bombs - Two Sorties

975   12/4/1979; Vic Wightman; Operation Racket - (Top LH corner of Zambia -as per Paddy Morgan's recollection); Hunter 1284; Ex

Vic Falls; Tony Oakley; Hunter 8116; Brian Gordon; Hunter 1258; Golf bombs & 30mm

977 14/04/1979; Vic Wightman; Mulungushi - Zambia ZIPRA camp; Hunter 1198; Golf Bombs; Chris's log book; Tony Oakley; Hunter 1284; JRT Wood - Page 327; Brian Gordon; Hunter 1258; Golf bombs

879 20/04/1979; Vic Wightman; Air Task – unknown; Hunter 1198; 30mm, 68mm; Input as per Tony Oakley logbook; Tony Oakley; Hunter 1286; Golf bombs; Brian Gordon; Hunter 1258; Golf bombs

980 21/04/1979; Vic Wightman; Air Task 917; Hunter 1198; 30mm, 68mm RP; Tony Oakley; Hunter 1188; Golf bombs; Brian Gordon; A/T 917; Hunter 1258; Golf bombs

981 22/04/1979; Vic Wightman; Hunter 1198; 30mm, 68mm; Brian Gordon; Hunter 1284; 68RP

983 26/04/1979; Vic Wightman; Op Grapple Air Task; Hunter 1198; 30mm; Tony Oakley; Hunter 1188;68mm; Varky Varkevisser; Hunter 1829; Golf bombs; Brian Gordon; Hunter 1284; Golf bombs

985 29/04/1979; Vic Wightman; Operation Oppress; Hunter 1258; 68mm RP; Tony Oakley; Hunter 1188; Golf Bombs

988 7/5/1979 Vic Wightman; Op sighting - Burma Valley VP7070? Hunter 1198; 30mm, 68mm RP 20mm; 26 Killed - Wind of Destruction - Page 532; Thrasher; Ginger Baldwin; (PB Page 531) Air Task unknown; Hunter; cannon

989 11/5/1979; Tony Oakley; A/T unknown; Hunter 1286; Golf bombs; Brian Gordon; Hunter 1188; Golf Bombs

990 12/5/1979; Tony Oakley; VP841612 Grain and buildings destroyed - JRT Wood Operations Table Bondage (External) Manica, Mozambique; Hunter 1188; 30mm, 68mm RP

991 13/05/1979; Vic Wightman; Hunter 1188; 30mm, 68mm RP; Tony Oakley; Hunter 1826; Golf Bombs; Brian Gordon; Hunter 1258; Golf Bombs

992 15/05/1979; Tony Oakley; Hunter 1284; 68mm Mantra; Brian Gordon; Hunter 1198; 68mm RP

994 17/05/1979; Vic Wightman; A/T 1148; Hunter 1286; 30mm, 68mm RP; Tony Oakley; Hunter 1198; 30mm, 68mm RP

995 20/05/1979; Vic Wightman; Hunter 1198; 30mm, 68 mm RP

113 28/05/1979; Tony Oakley; A/T 1223; Hunter 1821

996 29/05/1979, Vic Wightman; A/T 1232, Hunter 8116; 30mm cannon; Tony Oakley; Hunter 1188; Golf Bombs

1134 2/6/1979 ; Tony Oakley; A/T 1264; Hunter 1188; Golf Bombs

998 4/6/1979 Vic Wightman; Chivinge Tete Provence Mozambique; Hunter 8116; Golf Bombs; ZANLA killed; (External); Tony Oakley; Hunter ?; Brian Gordon; Hunter 1258; Golf Bombs

999 6-8/06/1979; J R Blythe-Wood; A/T 1475; Vampire FB9

1000 8/6/1979; Tony Oakley; A/T 1304; Op Tangent - Falls area; Hunter 1198; 68mm Mantra; No further details - log book inputs; Brian Gordon; Hunter 1284; 68mm RP

1135 8/6/1979; Tony Oakley; A/T 1319; Hunter 1198; 30mm, 68mm RP; Second sortie; Brian Gordon; Hunter 8116; 30mm, 68mm RP, Second sortie

1138 12/6/1979; Tony Oakley; A/T 1236; Hunter 1821

1003 22/06/1979; Vic Wightman; A/T 1392; Hunter 1188; Brian Gordon; Hunter 1284; 30mm, 68mm RP

1004 26/06/1979; Vic Wightman; A/T 1398; Op Carpet Air strike on ZIPRA camp at Chikumbi; Hunter 8116; Golf Bombs; 20 - 50 people killed. Martin Pearce – killed; Tony Oakley; North of Lusaka; Hunter 1188; Golf Bombs; JRT Wood - Pg 350/P-B Pg 534; (External); Brian Gordon; A/T 1401; Hunter 1198; Top cover

Operation Carpet was a two-pronged external attack by the Hunters on Zipra's Mulungushi training camp, combined with the SAS assault on the Zipra intelligence headquarters

1006 1/7/1979 ; Vic Wightman; A/T 1452; Air and ground attach on 100 tons of weapons, ammunition and Chicory munitions and supply depot. 30 - 35kms West; Hunter 8116; 30mm cannon; Varkie Varkevisser; Hunter 8122; 68mm RP; equipment destroyed. See P-B Pg 539; (External); Tony Oakley; of Lusaka; Hunter 1188; Golf Bombs; 2 sorties; Brian Gordon; Hunter 1821; Golf Bombs / Top Cover; 2 sorties

Operation Chicory is the airstrikes on the Zipra arsenal west of Lusaka

1008 7/7/1979; Vic Wightman; A/T 1474; Op Fiddle. Fire Force Zimbabwe Ruins; Hunter 1827; Dalmatian K-Car; Fiddle; Varkie Varkevisser; Hunter 1284; Golf Bombs; Tony Oakley; Hunter 8116; Golf Bombs; Brian Gordon; Hunter 1258; Golf Bombs; 10 terrs killed.

1009 8/7/1979; Vic Wightman; A/T 1474; Low level attack. Cabora Bassa **Op Cucumber** 6-9 July 1979; Hunter 1827; 30mm, 68mm RP; Cucumber; Tony Oakley; Mozambique; Hunter 1198; 1000 lb; (External); Brian Gordon; Hunter 1284; Golf Bombs, 1000 lb

1139 19/07/1979; Tony Oakley; A/T 1574; Hunter

1011 20/07/1979; Vic Wightman; A/T 1567; Cindy Plots. ZIPRA supply base on Zambesi near Livingston LL7750? Hunter 1258;

(External); Tony Oakley; Hunter 1198; Brian Gordon; Hunter 1188; 30mm, 68mm RP; 2 Sorties
1013 21/07/1979; Varky Varkevisser; Headquarters as briefed; Hunter 1188. Second sortie flown same day and third, ASR 1015, was flown on 23/07/1979.
1140 24/07/1979; Tony Oakley; A/T 1605; Hunter 1188; 30mm Matra
1016 26/07/1979; Tony Oakley; A/T 1617; Hunter 1188; Two separate air strikes.
1141 29/07/1979; Tony Oakley; A/T 1642; Hunter 8116; Frantan; Unusual Frantan target.
1017 5/8/1979 ; Vic Wightman; A/T 1677; Hunter 8116; 30mm, 68mm and; Tony Oakley; Hunter 1821; 68mm Matra
1142 7/8/1979 ; Tony Oakley; A/T 1693; Hunter 1817; Golf Bombs
1026 22/08/1979; (External); Vic Wightman; 6 targets known as Moscow; Interception by two Mig 19,s in Zambia; Hunter 1284' Golf Bombs; Tony Oakley; Hunter 1198; Golf Bombs; Brian Gordon; Hunter 1286; Golf Bombs, 1000lb - 2 Sorties
1027 22/08/1979; Vic Wightman; Zambia; Hunter 1286; Op Placid; Tony Oakley; Hunter 1198; Brian Gordon Hunter 1284; Golf Bombs
1029 23/8/1979; (External); Vic Wightman; Rufunsa and Solwezi (Qumbo's Farm, Placid Base); Hunter 1284; Golf Bombs; Tony Oakley; Hunter 1827; 30mm, 68mm RP; Ziggy Seegmuller; Hunter; Golf Bombs; Brian Gordon; Hunter 1286; Golf Bombs - 2 Sorties
Operation *Placid* and *Cucumber* – Hunter and Canberra airstrikes in Zambia, supported by SAAF Canberras 21 to 24 August 1979.
1031 26/08/1979; Vic Wightman; Hunter 1817; 30mm, 68mm
1032 2/9/1979; Varky Varkevisser; A/T 1827; Mozambique bridges100 kms inside Mozambique, Conbomune, SAAF helicopters based at Chipinda Pools , and helicopter Admin area established (External Op Uric); Hunter 1198; Golf Bombs; Tony Oakley; Mabalane, Barragem; Hunter 1816; 1000 Lb, Matra; Ziggy Seegmuller; Hunter 8; 30mm cannon; Brian Gordon A/T 1827; Hunter 1258
1035 5/9/1979; Operation Uric (External); Vic Wightman; A/T 1835 Mozambique bridges, Conbomune and Mabalane, Hunter 1284; 30mm cannon; Varky Varkevisser; Hunter 1188; 68mm RP; Tony Oakley; Hunter 1258; 68mm Matra; See ASR 1033; Ziggy Seegmuller; Hunter; Brian Gordon; A/T 1837; Hunter 1286; Golf Bombs; Guy Dixon; Hunter; Bell aircraft shot down at Barragem, Alex Wesson killed - KIA, SAAF Puma also shot down near Mapai the following day.

1036 5/9/1979 Vic Wightman A/T 1835; Uric (External) Air task 1835; Hunter 1284; Second sorties for 5 Sept. Varky - 2nd of Uric; Varky Varkevisser; Hunter 1188; three sorties; (External);Tony Oakley; Hunter 1258; Ziggy Seegmuller; Hunter; Brian Gordon; A/T 1837; Hunter 1286; Golf Bombs; 2 Sorties

1037 6/9/1979; Vic Wightman; A/T 1837; Uric (External) Air task 1837; Hunter 1284; 30mm cannon; Three sorties; Varky 2 sorties (ex Chiredzi; Uric; Varky Varkevisser; Hunter 1188; 68mm RP Buffalo Range) Tony Oakley - four sorties; (External); Tony Oakley; Hunter 1821; Golf Bombs; all Golf Bombs; Ziggy Seegmuller; Hunter; Brian Gordon; A/T 1837; Hunter 1286; Golf Bombs; 3 Sorties; Guy Dixon; Hunter.

1038 7/9/1979; Vic Wightman; A/T 1837; Uric (External) Air Task 1837; Hunter 1284; 30mm Cannon; Three sorties. Last in 1258; Uric; Tony Oakley; Hunter 1198; 68mm RP; (External); Ziggy Seegmuller; Hunter; Golf Bombs; Three sorties all with Golf Bombs
Brian Gordon; A/T 1837; Hunter 1286; Golf Bombs; 2 Sorties; Guy Dixon; Hunter

Op Uric/Bootlace took place between Malvernia and Chibuto in Mozambique, with SAAF air support with their Canberras, Dakota aircraft and with Super Frelon, Puma and Alouette helicopters. Hunter targets were mainly rail, road and river bridges over widespread areas of southern Mozambique. See Rhodesian Air Force Operations and Dr JRT Wood's map on the back cover. Hunter pilot Guy Dixon recalled: *"We initiated the strike at dawn on 5 September with eight Hunters using two 1,000-pound golf bombs each. Then we returned in pairs for the duration of the mission over the four days to provide top cover with 30mm cannons and 68mm Matra rockets. Our endurance with 230-gallon drop tanks was two hours 30 minutes, so we could loiter for about an hour over the target area. The brown jobs needed quite a bit of support. Actually, so did us blue jobs on Uric. We were outgunned; we had not seen organised anti-aircraft resistance like this before. I do remember taking a lot of gas from the 23-mm and 37-mm AA guns with the airburst ammo they were using. On 1 Squadron we had never seen so much flak before in the war on one target, especially the airburst variety. They were expecting us."*

1039 12/9/1979; Vic Wightman; Hunter 1821; 30mm, 68mm RP Two sorties; Brian Gordon; A/T 1838; Hunter 1817; 68mm RP

1040 13/09/1979; Varky Varkevisser; A/T 1926 Headquarter   Air
Task 1926; Hunter 1298; Brian Gordon; A/T 1926; Hunter 1284;
30mm Cannon
1041 14/09/1979; Vic Wightman; Hunter 1284; 30mm,68mm RP
1044 22/09/1979; Vic Wightman; Air Task; Hunter 1284; 30mm,
68mm RP
1143 23/09/1979; Tony Oakley; Air Task – unknown; Hunter 1286
1144 24/09/1979; Tony Oakley; Air Task 1938; Hunter 1284; 30mm,
68mm RP; Brian Gordon; A/T 1938; Hunter 1817; 68mm RP
1046 27/09/1979; Vic Wightman; Monte Cassino, Mozambique;
Hunter 1284; Op Miracle; JR Blythe-Wood; Hunter 1816;
(External); John Annan; Hunter; Ziggy Seegmuller; Hunter;
Brian Gordon; A/T 1974; Hunter 1258; Golf Bombs, 30mm; 2
Sorties; Brian Gordon   A/T 1976; Hunter 1821; 30mm, 68mm
RP; Brian Gordon; A/T 1974; Hunter 1198; 30mm, 68mm RP
1050 15/9/1979; Brian Gordon, A/T 1838; Monte Xilvuo relay station
in Mozambique; Hunter 1198; Norah; Hunter; (External)
1051 28/09/1979; Vic Wightman; Monte Cassino, New Chimoio;
Hunter 1284; Op Miracle; Ziggy Seegmuller; Hill 761; Hunter;
(External); Brian Gordon; A/T 1974; Hunter 1817; 30mm,68mm
RP; Brian Gordon; A/T 1974; Hunter 1258; 30mm, 68mm RP

1052 29/09/1979; Vic Wightman; Monte Cassino, Op Miracle; Hunter
8116; 30mm Cannon, 68mm; 2 Sorties; Vic Wightman; Hunter
1827; RP 435 x 30mm; Ziggy Seegmuller; Hunter; Brian Gordon;
A/T 1974; Hunter 1286; Golf Bombs, 30mm; Brian Gordon; A/T
1974; Hunter 1821; Golf Bombs, 30mm
1054 10/3/1979; Brian Gordon; A/T 2046; Chimoio - convoy of
vehicles close to Monte Cassino; Hunter 1821; 30mm, 68mm
RP; Brian Gordon KIA – Killed in action. See also PB's Winds
Op Miracle; Ziggy Seegmuller. Air Task 2046; Hunter; of
Destruction, Pg 556; (External); Tony Oakley; Hunter; Varky
Varkevisser; Hunter 1198.

A MIRACLE

Guy Dixon recalled the events of 3 October 1979 as follows: "I
was flying with Baldy Baldwin, my wing leader. We were flying a pair
of Hunters and were engaged in an interdiction run in Moçambique
after Op *Miracle*. We were called out on standby by the Brown Jobs
(Scout Willie van der Riet) who had spotted a target over the border in
Moçambique, and they thought it required investigation.

"Unbeknown to us, the SAS/Scouts had left "observers" in the
area to monitor the possible re-supply of the camps by the enemy after

our ground and air assault during Operation *Miracle* (targeting Monte Casino in Moçambique) the previous week. So, on observing vehicular activity in the area, the Brown Jobs called out a pair of Hunters to check out a convoy of vehicles in the area. It was October with shocking bush fire haze and very poor visibility. From Thornhill, Baldy and I routed via Umtali to initiate our "recon sortie" to the north. It was futile trying to spot anything at altitude due to the haze. To try and locate the target Baldy elected to take us low level in a loose battle formation at about 400 knots just north of Umtali, following the main Tete dirt road north. Baldy chose "fast" so as to give any ground fire some problems in tracking us. Good thinking Red 1!! However, even low level, at 400kts, with poor visibility and no horizon due to the bush fire haze and big mountains all around, spotting the convoy was all but impossible. Just trying to keep separation from each other and the ground was challenging enough while trying to look for ground targets. It was hot and also viciously turbulent, a rough ride low level.

"The Brown Jobs on the ground could hear the convoy opening fire on us each time we patrolled up and down the target area. So, the way we finally isolated the ground fire was to ask the spotters to tell us when the ground fire was starting, and when it had stopped, during our patrols. We then marked this on out maps and localized the search. On our third pass, finally, I sported the tracer fire directed at Baldy's aircraft. I told him he was being shot at and I had the target area visual. He handed me the lead and I then maneuvered to attack the target with 30mm cannon. Changing battle formation at that speed, in the haze while pitching up to perch height and trying to keep the target in sight was just about as challenging as the attack was itself. Not to mention we were surrounded by gomos (slang for mountain) that were hiding in the thick haze.

"Baldy spotted my strike and went in and delivered his own strike. We continued to attack the convoy in sequence. The convoys vehicles had now pulled off the road, split up and were scattered in the bush alongside the road. So, it was a case of 'spread em around' with our cannon fire in the dive as the convoy was now quite dispersed. The vehicles were only really vaguely identifiable by the tracer fire coming out of the bush and the haze. This really was the fog of war. It was all happening so fast, cannon fire from us, tracer from them, explosions from the ground, fear, adrenaline, burning vehicles, severe heat turbulence, constant uncomfortable G in a turn to keep the area in sight, radio jammed with chatter and thick haze. Just total overload and confusion as one tries to assimilate everything that is happening.

"All this done from the relative silence of a jet. What you see on the ground, you invariably don't hear in the cockpit. Bizarre. This was my 22nd Hunter strike of the war and in truth I was still very light in the pants as combat goes. No previous strike had even been vaguely similar, so I was just winging it, as I had no previous similar experience to draw on. As you can see by the date, 3 October 1979, I was 20. I got my wings a year earlier on 29 August 1978. As I put in my first strike on the target I can clearly remember Baldy's words to me during my training on the Hunter: "Remember Dixburger, it's not the bullet with your name on you must worry about, it's all those bullets with "to whom it may concern on," those are the ones that you have to worry about!!" Fine advice indeed.

"Ostensibly the convoy looked like (and was designed to look like) a re-supply convoy but in reality, when the vehicles pulled off the road and the tarps were pulled off, we realized this was an air ambush with heavy anti-aircraft artillery, 12.7, 14.5mm and possibly some 23 mm. Very little re-supply under the covers at all. We have been suckered in to this engagement and this was certainly the first "air ambush" of the war. The Brown jobs had almost completely withdrawn after Operation *Miracle* so there was no ground back up apart from the SAS/Scout observation posts. After 2 attacks each Baldy and I were very short of fuel and had to make a plan to start heading home. The low-level work trying to isolate the target had burnt much of our fuel.

Target marking Lynx – as flown by Mike Huson, who witnessed the Hunter going down, and the Canberras bombing run

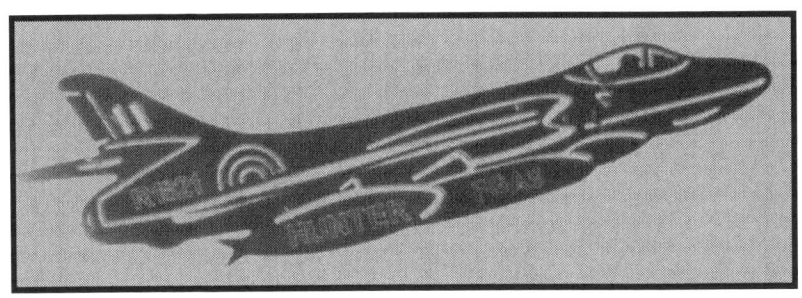

HUNTER - painted by Bill Sykes

HUNTER

*Dug out Gun-pits (above) and Covered Hide-outs (below),
Russian engineered*

Maingue / Monte Casino Defences

12.7mm Anti-Aircraft gun – mounted on a tri-pod

12.7mm Russian DshKM wheeled Anti-aircraft gun

Russian planned and engineered trench system – Monte Casino

23mm ZU-23 weapon

Trenches visible on Maingue – Monte Casino (kind favour Bob Manser)

14.5mm Russian Vladimirov KPU gun

23mm Unimog ZU-23

Note: this twin mounted ZU-23 on a motorised Unimog chassis. This heavy anti-aircraft cannon can be vehicular or static mounted.

"At this stage 2 more Hunters flown by Brian Gordon and Ziggy Seegmuller arrived overhead to relieve us. Baldy had to leave immediately as he was on minimum fuel for Thornhill, but Brian couldn't identify the target, so I said I would go in and mark the target for him, so we could get some continuity with the fresh pair of Hunters. Otherwise he would never find it in that haze with just a map. Baldy was just leaving the target area and told me to "let rip" with all the cannon fire I had left, as well as ripple fire on my remaining 68mm matra rockets - and then break for home.

"I released all my remaining armaments in the final attack to mark the target for Brian and turned for home. Brian confirmed that he had spotted my strike and that was my "green light" to leave, fast. (However, the final strike was one pass too many for me and by this stage I was critically sort of fuel for Thornhill, so I immediately diverted to New Sarum, landed and refueled there).

Brian Gordon - standing beside his Hawker Hunter FGA 9

"Brian turned in live and initiated the strike on the convoy and according to Ziggy, who was number 2 to Brian, 'There was a huge explosion when Brian was in the dive'. The confusion was such Ziggy wasn't even sure if a fuel or armaments truck hadn't been hit. He didn't think that it could have been Brian's Hunter, the invincible Hunter – never!

"Bottom line, Brian never came out of the dive. Whether Brian was shot, the aircraft shot down or had target fixation, we will never know, but he went in. That we do know. My own opinion is that ground fire was the more likely cause. Why do I say that? Firstly, because the amount of ground fire. (As Baldy would always say post op when asked how things went on the squadron, "well the flak was so thick we could walk on it" and chuckle ....) Secondly, the resistance was so fierce they sent a Canberra to bomb the target into "submission" in the afternoon. "Kevin Peinke and JJ Strydom was the crew. They too were shot down by the convoy's ground fire, (23mm?) and sadly both were killed. Heaviest Air Force losses of the war were that day. It was a very sad day for all of us. I only found out of Brian's demise when I got back to Thornhill after refueling in New Sarum. Baldy met me as I got out my aircraft and broke me the news. His exact words which I will never forget: "Brian has gone to the great big beer drink in the sky"

"That was just over 28 years ago, and the Brians wreckage has now finally been located. Great work indeed. History in the making – totally fascinating, and it sure brings back unbelievably vivid and indelible memories. As for war – look at Zimbabwe today and ask yourself was it worth it and what did they all die for? Oh, the futility of it all. War is the ultimate tool of politicians – pity it never has any real winners".

Ziggy Seegmuller was Brian's wingman, and this is his recollection when ORAFs broke the 'Hunter find's story. It brings further closure to the tragedy of 3rd October 1979.

"Politically, it seems the writing is on the wall; the Western powers have assembled against Rhodesia to find a quick fix to this thorn in their collective side. There is a definite feeling, especially amongst the civilian population, that time is now very limited for the present government. Many are already "taking the gap" (emigrating), and many more are starting to make plans to do so, most to South Africa, but some to UK and even further.

"On the military side, the war has taken on a new more intense phase; fighting is ferocious, almost in a conventional style at times, and whilst the kill ratio still remains at 20:1 in our favour, the numbers have increased dramatically – there is not a week that goes by without the loss of a dear one or a friend or acquaintance. The mood is one of concern, with many beginnings to wonder where this is all leading to. As a result, although morale is not low, it is certainly more serious and business-like, and much of the bravado that always characterized the forces' behaviour in the past is now wearing thin, hardly veiling the macabre reality lying beneath."

"In September 1979, security forces launched an almost conventional infantry attack upon the town of Mapai in Moçambique. A small town along the railway link to Maputo, Mapai was used by the terrorists as a staging point to launch cross-border raids into Rhodesia against farmers in the south-east, and then scurry back to the relative safety of Moçambique. Reliable intelligence backed up by photo-reconnaissance showed that the terrorists were amassing there, preparing for a major offensive. So, in September 1979, a large-scale combined forces pre-emptive strike was launched against the enemy. Although mainly a ground force conventional style operation, the Air Force was very active in the support role using Lynx a/c and Alouette helicopters ("G"-cars to ferry troops around the battle zone, and "K"-car gunships to soften hard targets with their superior 20mm cannon firepower).

"The enemy was very well dug-in indeed, and their fortifications and trench system network were well planned and defended with dozens of heavy machine gun emplacements – we were fighting terrorists who had been trained to expect such an attack and were prepared for it. Not the norm at all, where resistance would be fairly ineffective and short in duration, these guys meant business!

"On a number of occasions, we (No 1 Squadron Hunters) were called in to support troops that had been pinned down by enemy fire. On one such occasion, I recall being wingman to Squadron Leader John Annan (one of the Squadron's reserve pilots called in to help in times of high activity) when we had been called out to put in an accurate strike onto the pinnacle of a 300 feet high piece of granite we nicknamed "Monte Casino", from where an array of heavy machine-gun fire was taking its toll on our troops on the ground. When White Leader's bombs went one above and one below the target, affected by the interferometer arrangement we had on the 1000-pound "Golf bombs", there was some pressure on me to produce the goods! I steepened my dive angle a few extra notches to 65 degrees (the steeper the dive angle, the less gravity affects the trajectory of the bomb), and luckily my bombs landed plum on target! What happened next remains a blur in my memory: The Lynx spotter aircraft frantically reported that the gooks had broken ranks and had started scurrying in all directions along the top of the hill after the bomb attack many of them still dazed and confused from the huge concussions of those big bombs. The Lynx pilot urgently called us back into the target area as we were pulling out of the bombing attack profile, and we turned tightly to commence a 30mm cannon attack on them.

"This weapon can only be described as either totally exhilarating, or totally terrifying, depending on which side of it you happen to be on! The Hunter is equipped with 4 Aden 30mm cannons mounted within the fuselage, and each cannon has a rate of fire of 1200 rounds per minute. Each round has the explosive capacity of a small hand grenade. The pilot can select either two or four guns to fire, although the latter selection is specifically designed for air-air combat. On this day I selected all four guns to fire (that's 80 rounds per second!), and the effect of those High Explosive rounds on granite against a swarm of ant-like targets was devastating, oblivion for many.

"Some weeks later in Salisbury, I met up with a good friend of mine who had left his home in France to come and join the RLI to help fight our war. A mountain of a man, he saw me from a distance at the Oasis Motel, and he rushed up and picked me up and threw me into the pool, showering me with hugs and embraces (as the French are prone to do), shouting that I had saved his life on that terrible day – Mon Dieu, I couldn't have asked for more!"

"This attack on convoy story does not have a silver lining

"A few days later whilst the battle for Mapai raged on, we were once again called out, this time to attack a convoy of trucks proceeding to the battle zone. On this day I was paired with Flt Lt Brian Gordon, a great guy with awesome flying ability and with whom I shared the same birth date. The Lynx pilot, Flt Lt Mike Huson, had given us the target description on our way to the area, and when we got there, Brian instructed me to remain at 15 000 feet (above the range of small arms fire), whilst he delivered a rocket attack onto the target. This was not standard procedure, and I shall forever wonder if...

"Anyway, the convoy was not readily visible – they had heard us and had camouflaged themselves in amongst all the trees. As Brian entered the attack profile, I was positioned exactly in his 6 o'clock, which enabled me to see the rockets ignite in their rocket pods as he squeezed the firing button, very shortly followed by a huge fireball and explosion, as if he had hit a fuel truck in the convoy. Exuberantly, I recall shouting over the radio frequency in use, 'Good rockets, Brian!'

"I continued circling overhead at 15 000 feet, waiting for Brian to join up, but he never did. I called him on the emergency radio frequency repeatedly to no avail, eventually coming to the realization that maybe the explosion I had seen was not what I originally thought it was, and that maybe he had taken a hit.

"Eventually, approaching minimum fuel to return to base, and after brief discussion with the Lynx pilot, I put in an attack into the same area, delivering all my rockets in the hope of rustling out the enemy. I was also looking out for any signs of Brian's Hunter, but nothing was evident. Even stranger, there was no fire on the ground, as one would expect from an aircraft crash such as this. We never did recover Brian's body or the wreckage. However, months later, a photo was published in a terrorist paper showing what could well have been a piece of Brian's Hunter, claiming it had been shot down by 37mm anti-aircraft fire. The terrorists had planned this and had been lying in wait – it was a classic textbook ambush.

"Upon my return to Thornhill Air Base, still quite shell-shocked from the event, I was de-briefed by the Station Commander, asked if I was ok to continue, and then ordered to return to the same area to carry out another strike against the same convoy.

"Tragically, whilst we were re-arming and re-fueling on the ground, one of our precious Canberras, piloted by my good friend Flt Lt Kevin Peinke with Flt Lt JJ Strydom as navigator/bomb aimer, had attempted a low-level bombing run against the very same target that had already claimed one life, and had themselves been shot down with no survivors. I think that this was the worst day ever in the history of post WW2 Rhodesian Air Force.

"More importantly, it heralded the coming of a new type of war – one where the enemy was far more committed, better equipped, and better trained that we had ever seen before. Ironically, the politicians would put an end to it all just five months later."

Peter Petter-Bowyer wrote this conclusion in his *Winds of Destruction*: "Op *Miracle* had been successful but the cost to Rhodesia was unacceptably high. Two airmen and an RLI officer had been lost, together with an Alouette, in the high-density operation performed in direct support of Op Miracle. One Selous Scout was killed while clearing trenches on Day-One. Another was killed and three seriously injured on Day-Three when a captured weapon exploded as it was being made safe. Then on Day-Five the Air Force suffered the loss of three officers, a Canberra and a Hunter.

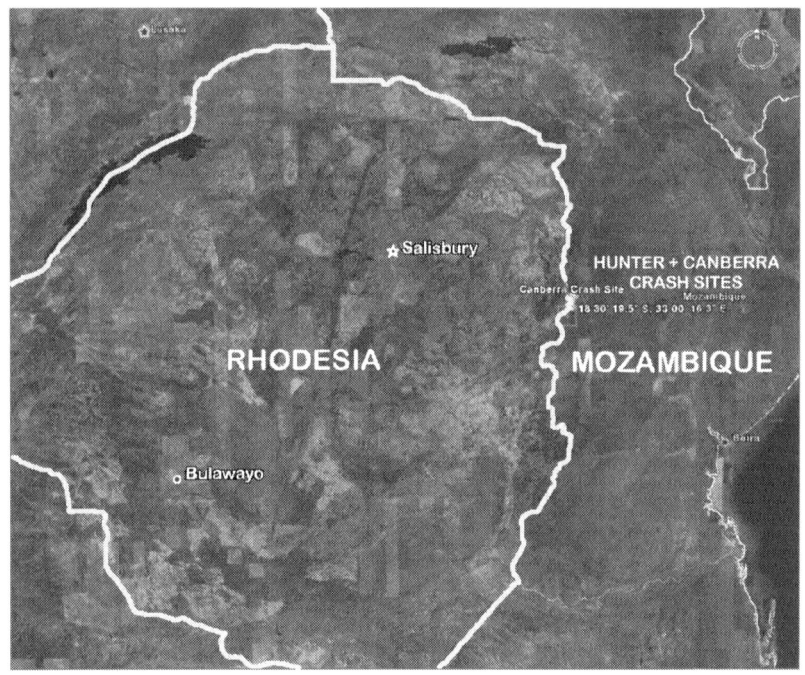

Selous Scouts Operation Miracle: 26 September 1979

By Peter Baxter History Blog

In spite of previous Rhodesian Security Forces successes against ZANLA bases in the Manica Province of Mozambique, it became evident from reconnaissance missions that camps had again been established in a sixty-kilometre radius from the town of Chimoio, not far from the Rhodesian border town of Umtali. Within this area, in what was now called the Chimoio Circle, and to the east of the Chimoio-Tete Road, aerial photographs revealed a large sprawling complex of five ZANLA camps. The whole 64 square kilometre area, named *New Chimoio*, was heavily fortified, with an extensive system of trenches and bunkers protected by heavy weaponry and anti-aircraft guns. ZANLA and their advisors had chosen a prominent 'bald' *kopje* to site a large force of men and anti-aircraft weapons to defend the camps below from air-strikes by the Rhodesian Air Force. The kopje was nicknamed *Monte Cassino* by the Rhodesians.

A Rhodesian artillery 25-pounder shelling the ZANLA positions at New Chimoio

Based on initial estimates of one to two thousand insurgents housed in the camps, ComOps (Combined Operations) made the decision to mount a ground and air attack on the ZANLA complex, using a flying column of one hundred troops from the Selous Scouts and the Rhodesian Armoured Car Regiment. Canberra bombers would initiate the attack, with Hunters and field guns of the Rhodesian Artillery providing heavy support as the assault progressed. One hundred paratroopers from 2 Commando, 3 Commando and Support Commando of the Rhodesian Light Infantry would be dropped east of the camp to put stop groups in place.

As a ploy to draw attention away from the real reason for this large gathering of troops, vehicles and aircraft near Umtali, RLI troops were deployed in mock fire force operations in the neighbouring TTLs, firing live ammunition to authenticate their presence.

It was however to prove a very costly deception, when a K-car carrying the Officer Commanding 3 Commando, Major Bruce Snelgar SCR (Post), flew into power lines. Bruce Snelgar, the pilot Air Lieutenant Paddy Bate and his tech Flight Sergeant Gary Carter all perished as Alouette R5705 crashed into the ground.

The Flying Column moves through the Honde Valley en route to Ruda

Under cover of darkness on 26 September 1979 the column, under the command of Captain Richard Passaportis of the Scouts, left Nkomo Barracks for Ruda Base Camp in the Honde Valley, just one kilometre from the Mozambique border. The convoy, which would pass through the Mutasa TTL, comprised Unimogs, Eland armoured cars with their 90mm guns, armoured troop carriers, the 25-pound artillery pieces, and the Scouts own armoured vehicle, the Pig. A bulldozer would be in place to assist with crossing the Gaerezi River (see my note at the end of this feature) into Mozambique. Large numbers of troops and helicopters had also assembled at Lake Alexander just north of Umtali.

Overall command of the operation would rest with Lt Colonel Brian Robinson and Wing Commander Norman Walsh of ComOps, from a Dakota overflying the area. At night, Lt Colonel Ron Reid-Daly would take over from his command centre on a nearby kopje. ComOps Tactical Headquarters would be based at the Grand Reef airbase, FAF 8.

It was planned that the flying column, together with the artillery, would enter Mozambique early the following day and set itself up at a burnt-out store, codenamed Madison Square, ready to follow the Canberra bombing run at 0700 hours. At this point near the target, the artillery would also be unlimbered and be ready to support the Air Force strike. At the designated hour, however, the column with the important artillery support was still waiting to cross the Gaerezi River.

The crossing onto Mozambique soil proved very problematic. Successive vehicles, weighed down with troops and war materiel, bogged down while attempting the river crossing. Eventually, the bulldozer had to individually drag each vehicle across, with the Puma APC-towed field guns being particularly awkward and resulting in them falling well behind in the column.

Eland armoured cars struggle to scale the slippery banks of the river into Mozambique

The twenty vehicles of the column had by this time become very fragmented, and as Canberras of No 5 Squadron were dropping their payloads over New Chimoio at the scheduled time of 0700 hours, most of the convoy was still stuck at the river crossing. By mid-morning, forward elements of the column had reached Madison Garden, but it was only by 1400 hours, seven hours after the Air Force bombing runs, that the main body of the convoy finally arrived at this staging post.

From Madison Square, the flying column of Scouts struck east, heading towards the road that would take them north to the camp. Arriving at the foot of Monte Cassino late that afternoon, the men were to spend an eventful night as the column was subjected to RPG-7 and 75mm recoilless rifle fire. While clearing trenches to secure their position, Trooper Gert O'Neill of the Selous Scouts was killed. The RLI stop groups, already in place, had an equally lively night, as fleeing insurgents stumbled into their ambush positions.

Come the following morning, further anti-aircraft defensive positions were identified on adjacent features, codenamed Hills 761 and 774, the latter being given the title Ack-Ack Hill. Flying through a cloud of flak, a Hunter strike from No 1 Squadron dropped sixteen 1000-pound Golf bombs on enemy positions, including Hill 774 which flanked Monte Cassino.

This allowed the Rhodesians to capture this hill which the defenders had vacated, taking their heavy weaponry with them. From this strategic point, Lieutenant Chris Gough and his men were able to direct mortar fire and Hunter strikes onto Monte Cassino.

On day three, Lieutenant Simon Willar's call-sign, with close-support from Hunters clearing his way, skirmished north towards Monte Cassino, clearing spot heights of ZANLA and neutralising their heavy weapons.

After successful questioning of an enemy capture, Captain Peter Stanton reported to Lt Colonel Tufty Bate of the RLI that information gleaned from the insurgent had provided a clear picture of what the attackers could expect at the top of Monte Cassino. With this in mind, further discussions were held with Richard Passaportis, leading to an infantry assault at 1000 hours. Two Selous Scouts troop call-signs led by Lieutenants Chris Gough and John Barnes, together with an RLI troop from 3 Commando commanded by Captain Bobby Harrison, began the challenging ascent. Chris Gough took the steep direct route, while the other two call-signs slowly made their way up the trench-latticed western route. Heavy supporting mortar fire was brought to bear on the top of the kopje immediately prior to the arrival of the Rhodesian troops. Elements of the Rhodesian Car Regiment had at this time also secured the adjoining Ack-Ack Hill.

The exhausted troops reached the top of Monte Cassino, finding it totally deserted. The Rhodesians now had strategic control of the base. Three soldiers were seriously wounded during the assault, and Trooper Ted Mann of the Selous Scouts was killed when a captured weapon he was trying to disarm exploded in his hands.

Chris and his men walked into a scene on top of Monte Cassino devastated by air and ground bombardments, littered with weaponry, supplies and other war materiel. The smell of dead insurgents permeated the hot air, but few bodies were actually found.

Evidently, most of the insurgents had withdrawn in what appeared to be a relatively orderly manner.

Rhodesian troops congregate at "Madison Square"

Twelve 44-gallon drums of sadza (maize-meal porridge, the staple of central and Southern Africa) attested to the fact that the base must have housed several thousand insurgents and camp-followers. The occupants had been drilled to evacuate eastwards and pick up the road to Chimoio.

There were numerous anti-aircraft emplacements scattered amongst a vast and elaborate system of trenches and bunkers, the weapons ranging from the Russian 12.7mm to 37mm. Large stocks of ammunition, tinned goods, food and medical supplies were also found.

That night, an RLI call-sign, Romeo One, positioned at a road block on the main road to Chimoio, saw a column of tanks and troop carriers approaching towards their position. As the Russian made tanks, backed up by what appeared to be a company of FRELIMO infantry came closer, Ron Reid-Daly, alerted to this fresh threat by radio, suggested to Richard Passaportis that Major Winkler move his Eland armoured cars into a protective cordon around Richard's Pig-based HQ, codenamed Hotdog.

Reid-Daly then guided the artillery onto the FRELIMO convoy. After five ranging rounds of gunfire, the next ten shells from the old British 25-pounders landed in quick succession amongst the attackers. The tanks immediately responded with some wild firing as they turned to flee the area. This was met by another salvo of shellfire from the Rhodesian guns, one round scoring a direct hit on a tank.

The FRELIMO rescue bid ended in a rapid withdrawal back towards Chimoio. Aerial reconnaissance the following morning revealed the FRELIMO column limping home, but before an air strike could be brought in, the convoy had camouflaged up in an area of thick bush, only moving out again when darkness fell.

On Sunday 30 September, the Rhodesians retired, leaving behind a few Scouts call-signs to monitor enemy activity.

A few days later, on 3 October, a large and heavily-armed Frelimo column was sighted. The Scouts call-sign, remaining concealed, reported that the column had fired with anti-aircraft guns on the now vacant Monte Cassino with great accuracy. As the column moved north towards Cruzamento, concern grew that their objective was to carry out an attack on the Security Forces base at Ruda, in retaliation for the attack on New Chimoio.

Air Force aircraft were scrambled to deal with the threat. At about 1300 hours, low-flying Canberras flew over the convoy, dropping Golf bombs. Canberra R5203, crewed by Flight Lieutenants Kevin Peinke and "JJ" Strydom, only released half of its bombs, so the pilot decided to turn and do a reverse run, but this fateful decision would cost them their lives as the enemy, seeing the aircraft turn and come back, had sufficient time to concentrate ground fire at the vulnerable bomber. The stricken aircraft, having lost both engines, had been coaxed to glide back across the border. Sadly, they did not make it, the Canberra crashing just short of the border, killing both men on board.

A while later, Hunter R1821, flown by Air Lieutenant Brian Gordon was also hit by ground fire, causing the aircraft to crash and kill the pilot. Whilst it was difficult in the thick haze for other aircraft to find the wreckage of the Hunter, it is known that Frelimo had discovered the site, as they had recovered what they could to display in a museum in Maputo.

The months of September and October 1979 were very costly in terms of human lives lost due to aircraft coming down during two Rhodesian cross-border operations, Uric and Miracle. Eighteen men of the Rhodesian Armed Forces and three of the South African Air Force died when their aircraft were shot down by enemy fire in Mozambique. Their bodies remained where they fell. A further three died in Rhodesia just as Op Miracle was about to be launched. A Canberra bomber, a ground attack Hawker Hunter, a Cheetah helicopter, an Alouette helicopter and a South African Puma helicopter were all destroyed.

A Rhodesian soldier inspects a Monte Cassino bunker

P. Baxter's Notes:

All the photographs that appear in this feature article are original Ministry of Information photographic prints which form part of Baxter's library. He has used four sources for his research; Ron Reid-Daly's Pamwe Chete, published by Covos Day in 2001; Beryl Salt's A Pride of Eagles, published by Covos Day in 2001; Alex Binda's The Saints, published by 30 Degrees South in 2007; and Peter Petter-Bowyer's Winds of Destruction, published by 30 Degrees South in 2005. Baxter found slight variations from one source to the next, but none were really significant.

There seems to be a question over whether the Frelimo tanks were T-34s or T-54s (they were T-54's). Also, and one Baxter would like to resolve, is the name of the river which the flying column crossed into Mozambique. All the literature gives it as the Gaerezi, but all the time while researching this operation, Baxter's brain was telling him that the Gaerezi is near Troutbeck. Reading PB's account raised that doubt again, as he refers to the Honde River, which to me is far more likely. Prof Richard Wood also says it is the Honde.

Dave Hughes

Peter...in my opinion the tanks were T-54/55's. I was the gunner in Eland 90 42A. (That's me in the photo crossing the Gaerezi River wearing a Second Chance bulletproof vest.) Our squadron along

61

with Major Winkler with his Unimog 2.5 mounting the .50BMG headed off the tanks at the access road during the night and then chased after them at first light using a Lynx overhead as a spotter. The tracks in the dirt appeared wider and of different configuration than those seen on the T-34 series. This observation was reinforced by the fact that we had already been training on our own T-54/55's at Inkomo (acquired from South Africa via Libya) when we were pulled off the course and back on to the Elands in order to conduct Op Miracle with the Selous Scouts. Considering that no one actually ever saw the tanks I think the spoor they left good evidence to conclude their model. Cheers!

Joe Boyum

Astounding story. I remember seeing it first in an encyclopaedia series called 'War in Peace'. This is without a doubt the most complete description of what is a brilliant bit of soldering.

Dave Hughes

Peter – not to nit-pick but you also omitted the first assault on Monte Cassino that was led by Maj. Winkler using his RhACR Support Troop Infantry. Ambushed by mutually interlocked A/A fire from the ZANLA defenders on top of the mountain Winkler's troops were pinned down and only able to escape thanks to the combined arms fire provided by the RhodAF Hunter jets – RLI 81mm mortar trucks in the Admin Centre – Rh Arty 25Iber's at Madison Square. It was a miracle that none of Winkler's men were killed…I remember listening in on Winkler's fire control directions on our Eland 90 radios – he was pretty calm and collected considering all the fire being directed at he and his men. It was only after night fell that all the members of RhACR Spt. Tp. Infantry were able to retreat off of the mountain and RV at the admin centre.

John Boulter

In fact, one got lost and he only came down the next day or something like that.

James Preece

Since studying the Bush War at Uni I've been fascinated by the conflict, and I have to say I'm extremely impressed with the professionalism and bravery of the Rhodesian Security forces. I'll definitely return to your website to read more of your articles. Thanks again!

I've just finished reading about operation Dingo which I thought was a very risky op, but this seemed even riskier! It amazes me that the Rhodesians managed to pull it off but I'm glad they did. Thanks for sharing your experiences and shedding more light on the subject.

Dave Hughes

L/Cpl Richardson and Lt. Sumpter were lost up on top of Cassino after the ambush – Richardson was wounded by grenade shrapnel in the buttocks – Sumpter unscathed. They worked their way back to the admin centre base camp in the middle of the night and made their way safely back.

David Merrett

The current Zimbabwean Government calls this the "Battle of Mavonde' and has produced some truly rubbishy "historical" (possibly hysterical) accounts of the action.

One, published a couple of years ago in the Zimbabwe Patriot newspaper (allegedly the result of eight months of research), claims that the Rhodesian forces tried to cover up this battle because they lost so comprehensively. Amongst other things, the article claims that "dozens" of RhodAF Canberras and Helicopters were shot down, and "several thousand" troopies KIA! It also implies General Wall was left totally demoralised by the "defeat".

Its staggering that after all this time, ZANLA/ZANU still has to indulge in this cheap, crappy propaganda to cover up for the poor showing of its fighters.

J Boulter

The guns went one short should have been 4 guns, second point was that the gun tower was over loaded due to having to many rounds on as no ammo vehicles went with the guns. A gun carries its basic needs 30 rounds the Ammo vehicle brings in the rest of the first line. Second the WO of the battery just returned to Arty after a long period did not go with the guns as he should have not his fault orders from people who don't understand Arty, To get through the mud and river the guns should have been hung off the trucks so taking the weight off the rear axle, Things like this happen when a new team steps in. One gun burst a barrel and a barrel was chopped in barrel replaced and the gun was back in action within 24 hours.

Rhodesian Light Infantry stop group east of Monte Cassino

The photo above is interesting as the "horns up" sign that two of these blokes on the left are doing was around back in those days. The single digit salute on the right has been around a long time!

Anti-aircraft weapons captured at Monte Cassino on display in Salisbury

Anti-Aircraft guns captured after the ZANLA tactical withdrawal

The photograph of the captured guns is acknowledged with thanks from Peter Petter-Bowyer (From Winds of Destruction, published by Trafford, 2003). Mike Huson, the Lynx pilot, reported that the three-barrelled 20mm guns were the first time that they had been used during the conflict - - and as such speculation that those guns could well have done most of the damage.

Felix Muchemwa and Paul Moorcraft accounts:

The Hunter flown by Air Lieutenant Brian Gordon was shot down and crashed just behind Monte Casino (north side), killing him since he failed to eject, writes Dr Felix Muchemwa in his book *The Struggle for Land in Zimbabwe* (1890-2010) that *The Patriot* serialised.

Day Two: On October 3, 1979, the second day of the raid, heavy ZANLA anti-aircraft fire inhibited precision bombing at 1 000ft. The Canberras were forced to drop their 1 000lb alpha bombs from the medium level bombing height of 15 000ft and they were ignored. Comrade Rex Nhongo had instructed ZANLA anti-aircraft gunners not to waste ammunition on aircraft flying above 5 000ft. However, the Hunters continued their dive-bombing manoeuvres, assaulting the anti-aircraft positions with 68mm rockets and 30mm cannon fire as well as golf bombs and, they met appropriate responses from ZANLA anti-air gunners. (Moorcraft and McLaughlin, 1982: p.116).

That morning, one Hunter flown by Air Lieutenant Brian Gordon was shot down and crashed just behind Monte Casino (north side), killing him since he failed to eject. (Jackson and Malsen, 2011: p.146 – the extract from the *Search for Puma 164* reads: "A month later on 3 October we lost a Hunter and a Canberra to AA fire on the same day – I was there when we lost the Hunter. Brian Gordon was killed in that accident and Kevin Peinke and J.J. Strydom were killed in the Canberra later that day).

Later on, the same day, the Canberra pilots, believing that ZANLA anti-air

gunners were not responding to Canberra bombings because they were scared came in lower than 5 000ft and the ZU-23mm anti-air gunners could not miss the large, darkish white targets and one bomber, flown by Flight Lieutenant Kevin Peinke with Flight Lieutenant J. J. Strydom as navigator was shot down and crashed outside Mavonde, killing both. (Jackson and Malsen, 2011: *The Search for Puma* 164 p.146).

The ZANLA forces, well dug-in, in the trenches on the northern part of Monte Casino, became apprehensive, fearing that the falling pieces and debris of shot down bombing jets might land on their positions. (Moorcraft and McLaughlin, 1982: p.117).

Still on the same day, about 40 of the Selous Scouts armed with FN and M16 rifles supported by the notorious NATO MAG guns and mortar 60mm, tried to assault the ZANLA HQ Base from the eastern slopes of Monte Casino Mountain, this time without the UNIMOG armoured cars.

The tortuous advance up the mountain, against well-armed dug-in ZANLA forces found the Selous Scouts being repulsed every step of the way up, and then eventually being pushed north-west of Monte Casino, unable to capture the mountain.

Remembering that stage of the battle, one of the Selous Scouts later admitted: "We knew then that we could never beat them. They had so much equipment and there were so many of them. They would just keep coming with more and more." (Moorcraft and McLaughlin, 1982: pp.165-166).

ZANLA 'machine gun and mortar fire against the Selous Scouts advance was well controlled and accurate'. (Cole, 1984: p.357). The Selous Scouts had to be airlifted by helicopter back to their temporary HQ on the eastern side of Monte Casino. In the process, an Alouette III helicopter K-Car was shot down. (Moorcraft and McLaughlin, 1982: p.117).

Throughout the night on the second day of the fight, the artillery duel of the first night was repeated, only this time, the bombardment started from the Rhodesian Selous Scout HQ, east of Monte Casino and it was not intended to knock out any target. Rather, it was meant to keep the Zanla guerrillas fully awake and harassed the whole night, thus wearing them down to a point of being unable to resist further assaults. (Nhongo).

Day Three: On the third day of fighting, much of the excitement on both sides had subsided and caution prevailed. The Canberras were back to the safe 15 000 to 21 000ft altitude and were deploying both the 1 000lb alpha bombs and the 500lb napalm bombs to carpet-bomb Mavonde in a 'scorched earth' strategy. Everything inside the Mavonde ZANLA HQ Base had to be pulverised by the alpha bombs whose toxic emissions were further expected to suffocate ZANLA forces in their trenches and bunkers. However, the Canberras were completely ignored and met with total silence from the anti-air gunners. Cde Nhongo's standing order was still not to waste ammunition on aircraft flying beyond 5 000ft. Therefore, it was only the Hunters' diving manoeuvres that 'drew curtains of flak from the (ZANLA) anti-aircraft positions on the hilltop and in the trenches. (Moorcraft and McLaughlin, 1982: p.116).

And on the whole, it was the musasa trees rather than the ZANLA forces in the trenches and bunkers that suffered the bombing. But there was still no rest for the fighters because the interludes between aircraft strikes were always well-filled in by the artillery barrages.

A surprise Frelimo intervention with T54 tanks in the afternoon disrupted the routine of the fighting. The Frelimo T54 unit advanced into the Mavonde Zanla HQ Base, from the eastern side of Monte Casino, guided by Comrade Moffat (Masabeya), a Zanla member of the General Staff and permanent medical representative at the Chimoio Hospital. The reinforcement was immediately challenged by the Rhodesian 25-pounder guns and the Eland armoured cars' 90mm guns and the ensuing duel went into the night in which Frelimo tactically retreated back to Chimoio, having been outgunned. (Cole, 1984: p.357).

By midnight on the third day of fighting, Zanla (critically anti-air gunners and Comrade Belingwe's mortar 82mm battery) had exhausted their ammunition and Commander Nhongo ordered a tactical retreat. (Nhongo). Comrade Belingwe was ordered to give cover to the retreating ZANLA forces by keeping the Rhodesian artillery busy.

The anti-air guns were dismantled for easy transportation and wheeled out. So were the recoilless guns. Senior members of the Zanla High Command and General Staff were assigned command duties to lead the 6 000 strong Zanla force in large, battle-ready fighting formations out of Mavonde, many strong positions being held up until the right moment to withdraw. (Moorcraft and McLaughlin, 1982: p.117).

Front squads were not to engage the enemy unnecessarily to avoid night battles since Rhodesians not only had night vision equipment but also had developed night fighting capability. Against the orderly fighting retreats, the RLI, sitting in their ambush positions could not (without air support) dare challenge the heavily armed Zanla forces and, consequently, there were extremely few and unsustainable contacts during the withdrawal.

Hunter pilot Air Lieutenant Guy Dixon is quoted as saying "I was there when we lost the Hunter. Brian Gordon - - "

MANSER / PEINKE CONNECTION

The reason for Bob Manser's interest is that he was trying to locate Kevin Peinke's Canberra crash site. Bob is a radio fitter off No 16 Course, who fondly remembers Kevin choppering him as a TF ex-Regular on Cashel Valley assignments. They got to know each other when Bob was on TF call up and found Kevin a very cheerful chap, full of fun and bounce and always had time for a chat. Bob runs a history/environmental society which included organising an over-land trip to Senna on the Zambezi, the site of Mary Livingstone, nee Moffat's grave.

Bob had heard from farmers in the area that some of the locals vaguely remember the air crash, but after 30 years, memories are fading rapidly. Any metal is a valuable commodity. It is thus not surprising that not much, if any, would have remained after the Canberra crashed. Bob commented: "If I do locate the place, I do not expect to find much in the way of wreckage as all metal here is like gold and chopped up and sold to the metal collectors who scavenge the country-side buying up anything, all sent back to China". Most of the locals in Manica Chimoio area speak Shona (rather than Portuguese), and this may aid Bob in locating the exact site.

Local Manica town historian of note, James "Tackie" Bannerman, kindly supplied the Moçambique maps, which helped to establish where the Canberra and Hunter crash sites occurred, in order to assist Bob Manser in his search. Take note that what the Rhodesians called Monte Casino is in fact called Maingue by Moçambique.

The riddle was further solved when ex-Selous Scout Willie van der Riet e-mailed the writer and had this to say: "I was on an OP to the north west of Monte Casino, observing the FRELIMO convoy being attacked by the Air Force. Peter Curley was with me. I can confirm that the Hunter went down at the junction of the two roads – marked Mavonde Aldeira. The FREDS (Jargon for FRELIMO and / or Russian advisors) had stopped firing and possibly a minute or so had gone by before I heard the Canberra going down to the north of my position.

Peter Petter-Bowyer, serving in ComOps at the time, was of immense value in re-constructing the events leading up to, and actions taken, with the loss of the two strike aircraft. Comops concluded that the FRELIMO columns were headed for a retaliatory assault against the Ruda Base in the Honde Valley – which is why ComOps has reacted to Willie's OP observations.

Immediately prior to going to print, I received the following e-mail from Bob: "My mate Barry Meikle went to a braai yesterday and mentioned our quest for the missing planes to our friend here, Porky Christie-Smith. Porky works for Moçambique Leaf Tobacco (Universal Tobacco) and is in charge of thousands of small-scale farmers in Manica. He told Barry that his men have often told him that there is still the tail plane of a Ndege in Manica. Porky has not seen it himself but knows the spot. I am sure if we find one, through Porky's vast African farmer network we will find them both". The mystery of this 'ndege tail plane' remained unresolved.

THE SEARCH FOR THE CRASH SITE OF THE HUNTER
lost during Op Miracle, October 1979 - By Bob Manser

As I now live in Chimoio, Manica Province, Moçambique, I have been keen for some time to locate the exact crash sites of the Hunter of Brian Gordon and the Canberra of Kevin Peinke and JJ Strydom (killed in action on 3 October 1979).

I was not sure where to start but having had chats with various ex-Scouts friends plus many chats with Prop and also help from PB and other ORAFs members I had a fair idea where to look, give or take a few hundred square kilometres! Feedback from local farmers and other folks' resident in Manica helped, plus also intrigued by vague stories that local tribesmen knew of the incidents that occurred nearly thirty years ago and had varied ideas as to where the remains of the aircraft were.

Luckily a few weeks back my two friends – Pedro Swanepoel and Richard Quinell - who work for a SA based forestry company offered to take myself and co-searcher, Barry Meikle on a tour around Monte Casino as it was all part of their forestry area. We started off from near Manica town and headed up the old Tete, Mavonde road looking for the elusive crossroads and the village called "Cruzamento" which translated means crossroads, all a bit confusing. After some hours of working our way up to the Pungue and back down the power line tracks on the east side of Monte Casino we drew blanks. Every indigenous we spoke to had not heard of any crashed planes: especially all those years ago.

We backtracked to the old Tete road again and stopped at various crossroads and hailed any bystander we could find seeking information. Mick Hamence will chuckle at this as I always carried the book on Canberras by him and Winston Brent and showed the cover to any local we chatted to, hoping we may find one who may have had seen something similar in years gone by.

About 50 metres east of the road virtually in the centre of the village we came across a smallish depression in the ground and the remains of a turbine. The crash site was very close to the road, maybe 40 or 50 metres in, just behind some small shops.

We scrabbled around under the turbine and discovered about ten 30mm Aden gun "doppies" and a few rusty 30mm H/E heads. Many of the doppies still had un-burnt black cordite like granules in them. I reckon the 30mm shells certified the crash site as the one of the Hunter.

CANBERRA

Mick Hamence and Winston Brent's book of the Canberra as used by Bob Manser to show to the local village inhabitants

Brian's Hunter FGA 9 – R1821

Cruzamento village and cross-roads – the Hunter crash site (behind and in between the huts that can be seen). Permission to enter was needed

Barry Meikle and Bob Manser with a 30mm case and Hunter engine turbine compressor disc's

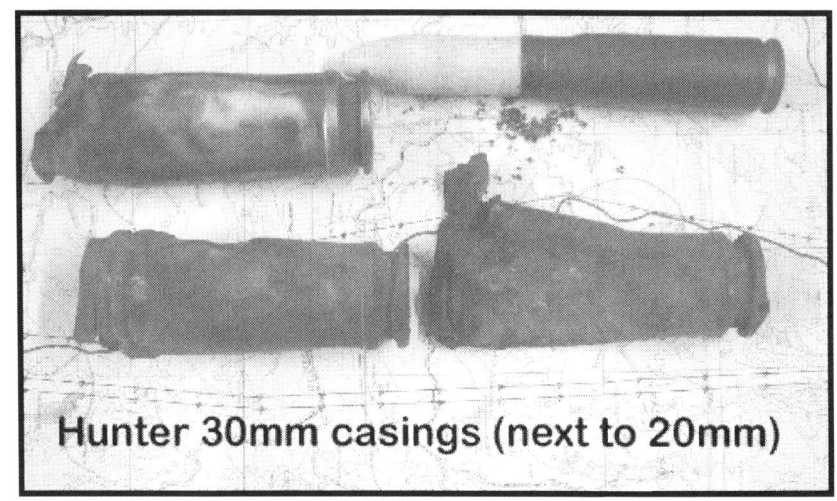

Hunter 30mm casings (next to 20mm)

The Gordon Hunter crash site and remains of the turbine

Cordite still in 30mm cannon shells

Barry Meikle and Bob Manser holding Brian Gordon's 30mm cannon shells recovered at the Hunter crash site – Cruzamento village.

Remains of Hunter wreckage, possibly the jet-pipe – still lying in the depression at the crash site

We were disappointed in the lack of wreckage, but it must be remembered that most of it was taken away by FRELIMO and put on display in Maputo.

The GPS co-ordinates are South 18degrees 34' and East 33 degrees 01'.

Another interesting fact is that the officious gents had heard of another crash site to the northwest, and said an aircraft was supposed to be in the foothills just on the border with Zimbabwe near a village called Ndanga; this must be the Canberra site.

We had run out of time that day, but my forestry mates have promised us a jaunt in their sturdy Toyota Land cruiser next month when they visit that area to pay wages so hopefully, we will eventually discover the Canberra wreckage.

It is a small world as a few weekends ago I trekked up to the Zambezi to see Mary Moffat's grave, wife of David Livingstone and on the way back popped into the bush camp and sawmill of Ant Whites and chatted to him about our planned search. He could not help though, as he was not involved in Operation *Miracle*. However, a day later into my office comes my mate of old, John Barnes who was returning from a brief holiday to the coast. He was actively involved in

Miracle and was busy extracting his team from Cruzamento when the aircraft incidents occurred, so I got some first-hand info from him.

All in all it was a great team effort and many thanks go to my Chimoio mates Pedro, Barry, Richard and all at ORAFs who helped in this search.

Many years ago my wife taught at the Sir Roy Welensky Junior School in Dete and one of her young pupils was a Brian Gordon (this was subsequently confirmed as correct).

B Manser
Chimoio 27/10/07

All credit goes to Bob for this terrific achievement, for the resolute tenacity and drive to persevere in order reach the objective. Well done Bob, I am sure we all salute you. I also need to acknowledge all the fine photographs (that in themselves speak a thousand words) and many maps which helped one to appreciate the enormity of the task.

I believe some special words of thanks are in order. To Eddy Norris for putting many interested bodies in touch with one another. To Kevin Tidy (the engineer who constructed the Chimoio Memorial) who flew Bob around Maingue / Monte Casino in his Cessna 182 aircraft. Thanks to local historian James 'Tackie' Bannerman who supplied maps of the areas. To Barry Meikle for his enthusiastic support for Bob. Pedro Swanepoel, who speaks Portuguese fluently, an essential team-member together with fellow forester Richard Quinell. Peter Petter-Bowyer was particularly helpful for pointers to Cruzamento village in his e-mails and his descriptions in *Winds of Destruction*. Willie van der Riet's reminisces was riveting – he was sitting on a gomo at the time!

Tony Oakley gave first-hand accounts of the appalling weather conditions prevailing – plus a good write-up in Pride of Eagles. Big Kutanga Mac John McKenzie for edging everyone on, especially me! Thanks also to Bruce Harrison for his evaluations, and particularly his influence and involvement in the Rhodesian Forces Memorial Project.

Readers may well be interested in the comments received so far. Tony wrote: "What a marvellous achievement, thank you for your fortitude and perseverance. The loss of Brian, on what was a very troublesome target, was a sad loss indeed. I have written to Prop before on this incident; Beryl also has some material in her book, for up until this point, the Squadron had achieved remarkable successes against very hostile targets without loss of life. It was an accepted fact that the Hunter was invincible, how could this have happened? I am pleased there can now be some closure on this sad event and would also appreciate pictures or maps as they become available. Thank you all once again for your sterling efforts and I look forward to hearing that you have been as lucky with finding the Canberra".

Willie wrote: "Fantastic news, a moment in time brought back, well done Bob and team, please keep me in mind when you have the photos. Pamwe Chete".

Bill Sykes added: "I have read all the letters of praise for your efforts and cannot better those sentiments. Congratulations indeed. Wouldn't it be great if you have as much success with the Canberra? And what a story for the next Bateleur ..." (Bill published the full story in the April 2008 edition of Bateleur. His editorial read "Bob Manser must be singled out, and congratulated, for his tenacity in searching and finding, against all odds, the remains of the Hunter and Canberra that were lost in Moçambique in 1979. No-one ever expected them to be discovered. This puts to rest these two incidents and closes the final chapter of the bush war").

PB wrote: "Amazing after 28 years to see Brian Gordon's unfortunate death site. Copied to Vic Wightman who was his OC. No doubt you will pass this to Eddy Norris when he returns to RSA. He will pass it on too many who will be very interested."

Graham Patterson, in Australia, wrote: "I have maintained a motivation to seek something further for these people, apart from being Bluejobs; it is also that they deserve some form of memorial. I am incredibly proud of their sacrifice and that we all served together. I do know Bruce (Harrison) and would make some form of donation to the project, but would wish to see if any other groups would wish to take something further on and try to obtain the info of their resting place and if possible erect a memorial".

Al Thorogood wrote: "I still remember the day well even after all these years and it was of my personal low points. Especially as it occurred exactly a week after a K Car crashed killing Paddy Bate, Gary Carter and Bruce Snelgar - I saw them go in and had a medic on board so went to land and assist only to fly under the wires he hit(without seeing them either!). A week later after a fairly busy time! We had word at Grand Reef that Brian had gone in and were scrambled with Willy (?) Joubert as my tech. We went to a Rebro just on the border to learn of the loss of the Canberra as well - we were tasked with S&R. We were unable to locate Brian's crash site as things were a tad warm around the area still and there was still a reception committee waiting, however we did locate the second site at OS map coordinate WQ 008543. . We landed at the site and sadly could confirm no survivors - Kevin still had a load of Alphas on board when he went down. A tragic loss of all I too still salute you all as well. Gone but certainly not forgotten."

-o-O-o-

Eddy Norris also complimented Bob Manser - "Stand Tall" my Friend. You are "True Blue." Sincere thanks for your wonderful achievement and for your friendship. Thanks also must go to all that were involved on this project.

Michel (Ziggy) Seegmuller: "I took great interest in the story of how you succeeded in discovering the crash site of Brian's Hunter - true perseverance indeed - well done!!! I was Brian's wingman on that dreaded 3rd October in 1979, and I have included a recounting of the events of that day out of my memories for your info. Funnily enough, Brian and I shared a birthday on November 15th, he is a year older than me, and we were good drinking buddies! About 10 years ago, I spoke with his parents who moved to Sedgefield in SA"

-o-O-o-

John McKenzie was so impressed with the poem composed by Gary Albyn that he decided to not only incorporate it in the Miracle Memorial, but persuade Garry to compose the second poem of a Canberra as well.

THE HUNTER – Poem by GARY ALBYN

The hangar mutes the muffled sound
Of airmen recently arisen,
The sun is yet to cleave the ground
With the flush of its early prism.
A sulphur glow
Bathes the floor below
And illumes in menacing fashion
There parked abeam
In battle scheme
The theme of an airman's passion.

Onto the apron with stately grace
The teams tow out the 'planes
The pride and joy of this airbase
Veterans of many campaigns.
With an imposing air
You're made aware
Of the Hunter's grace and beauty,
But don't be charmed
Or easily disarmed
For she knows her centurion duty.

I enter a zone that the pilot knows
A place of heightened senses
Spirits soar and awareness grows
And I shed my common pretences.
We share a bond
Above and beyond
A place of high esprit
Where laws that decide
That airflow provide
The lift that sets us free.

I focus my mind as I near the jet
Lines like a Spartan blade.
Against the sky a silhouette
Ready for an aerial crusade.
I pay respect
To cause and effect
By checking her thoroughly,
For corners shaved
Is false time saved
An invite for catastrophe.

My nostrils flare with the tainted smell
Of oil and cockpit sweat,
As I strap in tight to my airborne shell
And run my pre-flight check.
Fire ignition!
Commencing mission!
As the needles all start to settle,
I wave cavalier
To the ground engineer
And warm up the Avon's metal.

She's lined up now on the centre-line
Straining against the brakes,
I stoke the fire and hear the whine
As she flexes, arches and shakes.
Cleared by tower
Fistful of power
She exits like a racehorse,
I feel the crush
And the adrenaline rush
And thank God I joined the Air Force.

I touch the brakes then lift the wheels
The drag gets packed away,
This is how a raptor feels
When it is hunting for its prey.
I scan the sky
With practiced eye
And look-out for a sign.
That there's another . . .
A flying brother . . .
Who soars on wings divine.

Gary Albyn © 2006

A HUNTER WAS LOST - Poem by MATTHEW BLACKLEY

In a Rhodesian sky
Hunters flew
High above
In the blue

With speed and courage
Down, they streaked
Unleashing
All of its' fury
On the enemy

A masterpiece of design
Flown by the chosen few
A Hunter was lost....
In seventy nine

We could not effect..
A recovery...

81

All that did belong
To a family
To a squadron

So many years
Have passed
Since that terrible day
So many tears

Never again will we hear
That special Hunter sound
Flown by Brian
It does not matter
For now...
He is found
                    Matthew Blackley 2007

Bob Manser found the Brian Gordon Hunter that crashed in Moçambique twenty eight years ago, in November 2007. This phenomenal news was just too late for a Forces promotion in Johannesburg that coincided with the Annual Memorial service held 11th November every year – a date which is so sacred to most Rhodesians.

There is indeed a <u>right</u> time for everything (Solomon, Eccl 3:1). John Kutanga McKenzie was jumping up and down in Swaziland. Eddy and Trish Norris were in Canada, visiting their daughter Denise and ex-7 Squadron technician Shumba Taylor. Eddy, of notorious ORAFs fame, was trying to take a well-earned break from the ever-demanding keyboard affecting his health. But all credit goes to Eddy in recognising that the Manser achievement was once again world headline news to thousands of folks in all corners of our planet. Bob's original aim was to try and find the Canberra because of the connection Bob enjoyed with his close friend Kevin Peinke.

With Eddy's news flashes congesting cyberspace, reports from all over came flooding in. Eye-witnesses of the Hunter and Canberra crashes came to the fore. I even got a fascinating report from well-respected RLI Fire Force Commander Rick van Malsen who not only was with the Peinke crash search and rescue attempt, but also came across the Ian Donaldson Canberra crash site (with navigator David

Hawkes and Selous Scout / ex SAS Rob Warracker) in the Malvernia area. Readers must realise that the remains of our heroes here mentioned and killed in action were never recovered. Close relatives may not forgive me for digging up old bones - - but for many more others it will at long last bring closure so that souls may rest in peace – on this 11th Day of November 2007 – the very day I now write this but more so a day very worthy to commemorate the unveiling of the Rhodesian Forces Memorial at the Dickie Fritz Shellhole in Edenvale.

Then the miracle happened – Bob Manser and his very good friend Barry Meikle (cousin of Brian Meikle) found the remains of the crashed Kevin Peinke Canberra exactly 7.05 kilometres (only 3 odd nautical miles) north of the Hunter crash site – three days after the eleventh hour, of the eleventh day, of the eleventh month – 2007. May our fallen heroes without decent, identifiable graves, now have a final resting place.

The following report and pictures speaks volumes. The maps set the scenes, Bobs spiel follows and captions to Bobs photographs tells the story.

SAM - 7 Strela / Grail Surface to Air heat-seaking missile

Anti-Aircraft SAM-7 heat-seeking missile

Soviet soldier taking aim with SAM-7

Barry's persistent negotiations with the local inhabitants

Eve's Toes – prominent feature on the Zimbabwe border

Crossing the Honde River at a low water drift

Crash site – measuring 30 metres wide x 60 metres long

OLEO – the leg and axle that carry the main-wheels

Avon Turbine compressor rings – with all turbine blades
sheared off. Note angle centre shaft bent

Engine remains – combustion chambers

Stator blade nozzle for the turbine and second oleo

Canberra undercarriage / Oleo leg

Turbine ring gear

The locals making peace with the Spirits, before leaving the crash site. They also revere and remember the past conflict. Everyone had to crouch and clap hands – to tell the Spirits that one was present

"We took various photographs and got the GPS co-ordinates of the site but before we left Barry held a small service. He spoke a few words of prayer for Kevin and J.J and I placed a small cross and remembrance Poppy by the turbine.

These were Barry's words: "With thanksgiving let us remember Kevin Peinke and J.J. Strydom who sacrificed their lives so that we may live on in peace, and in appreciation we now dedicate this cross to their memories. Help us to keep them in our thoughts and never to forget what they gave for us".

We then recited together that well known First World War poem (Robert Graves / Wilfred Owen?)

They shall not grow old as we that are left grow old
Age shall not weary them, nor the years condemn
At the going down of the sun and in the morning
We will remember them.

"The locals then asked us to crouch whilst they repeated their ceremony; they said it was to tell the spirits we were now leaving.

"Again, a hot weary trek back to the bakkie but we had achieved our objective. We said cheers to the policeman and the others and gave the police fellow some money to dish out to the guide and his subdued father who was looking decidedly seedy after his longish trek in the midday sun, his previous heavy intake of hooch couldn't have helped!

"Don't know if they got a fair share of the handout, who argues with a cop with an AK? We then returned to Cruzamento and the Hunter site where Barry carried out a similar service to the one he had recited at the Canberra. We did not leave the cross behind here as it would have been taken away in no time. The people here did not seem to have the same respect or reverence as the villagers at the previous site. , I suppose because it was in the middle of a busy village shopping centre.

"Many thanks must go to Barry Meikle as his input into this search was immense, without his help I doubt if I could have made it happen. We had attained what we had set out to do right in the beginning, located the two sites and also obtained accurate GPS co-ordinates for future reference.

Canberra 183019.5 330016.3.
Hunter 183402.5 330112.6

"Thanks must also go to Eddy Norris, Prop Geldenhuys and Tackie Bannerman for all their help, advice, and prodding to get the job done and to other members of ORAFs who helped in anyway. I personally think that we can now close the chapters on these two tragic events of 28 years ago. I also feel that Barry's few words of prayer at both sites brought a touch of spiritual peace to these rather sad places.

"What about the Canberra that went in down Malvernia way? Well, maybe a search next year."

Bob Manser, Chimoio

WORLDLY FEEDBACK REPORTS

The news was flashed across the globe by Eddy Norris and a magnificent response by no less than 107 people from all walks in life lauded Bob and Barry on their phenomenal achievement.

Crash site co-ordinates are:

❖ Brian Gordon Hunter – GPS 18°34'02.5" South 33°01'12.6" East
         - WQ 023473
❖ Kevin Peinke Canberra – GPS 18°30'19.5" South 33°00'16.3" East
         - WQ 008542

Eye-witness accounts were received from:

❖ Willie van der Riet – Selous Scout positioned on the OP.
❖ Ziggy Seegmuller – Wingman to Brian Gordon.
❖ Al Thorogood – Alouette helicopter pilot who inspected the Canberra crash site.
❖ Mike Huson – Lynx pilot
❖ Paul Perioli – Canberra Bomb Aimer / Navigator
❖ Gavin Wehburg – took photographs of the Canberra crash.
❖ Bob Manser and Barry Meikle, who found both sites 28 years after the event.

The following dossier compiled by Eddy Norris is reproduced below with all humility.

Orlando Anibal (Ex R Troop) - It is a true saying "Rhodesians never die!" The memory of those who gave their lives will never be forgotten. I have fond memories of seeing our Hunters.

Captain William Anderson RAAC [Retd] - Australia - You all make me proud who fight together for what is right. God Bless

John Blythe-Wood - The efforts of all involved are greatly appreciated, no less by me, and bring back so many memories. I look in my log book and see that Op Miracle started on 27 October 79, and at the time I was O.C 2 Squadron but current on Hunters. I see I flew in R1816 on 27th September and again in R1258 on 03 October, on air task 2046, on the fateful day. Memories are dim, but I seem to recall being called out to fly as Baldwin's # 2, and we ended up firing rockets. I remember the haze was very thick and the target acquisition was very difficult.

Hugh Bomford – New Zealand - Well done to all concerned

Mike Botha, Australia - An awesome achievement guys! Rhodesians will NEVER forget all those who gave their life for the gutsiest country the world has ever seen.

Dave Bourhill. - Thank God we are still looking for our comrades, it brings back many proud moments but also so many sad moments. I saw all the aircraft flying overhead to the OP area without me, so that may have been my lucky day.

Shirley Briggs (nee Dyke, born at Eiffel Flats, Gatooma 1933) - Because of people like this, brave honest, stalwart and true. Rhodesians will live on in history as they deserve to do. I am an Oldie now, but I will never forget the great heart of the Rhodesian heroes who fought for us all. Today you will see us...all over the world we have spread ourselves, but we are still here ...and we will always remember...and feel that binding spirit that made us what we are. Go well! Our brave people. Humba Gashlie

Angela Cohee - "Rhodesians Never Die" is very true, when this incident happened my Dad (in the BSAP), was absolutely devastated, as were we all. Thank you so much for taking the time and effort in finding their crash site.

Geoff Dartnall - Congratulations to Bob on an amazing job well done. All the very best to you - keep up the good work- to yours and all those sufficiently interested in recent history.

Guy Dixon (UAE) - I was there on that fateful day in one of the 2 lead Hunters that identified the target and initiated the attack before Brian Gordon arrived on the target.

Mara du Toit - Thank you for this account of a search that proves again how important comradeship is and that lost friends are never forgotten (Mara compiled the RFMP Roll of Honour rolls for the Memorial).

Mike Edden, (BSAP) Australia - Congratulations on a job well done. Saw Chimoio and Tembue with my SB team first raid 1977. Was at ComOps '77 - '80 and was deeply saddened when the planes went down. Have seen Norman Walsh recently and remember Peter PB from ComOps. Glad to see that the RhodAF has been honoured this way, a great force of men I was proud to have served with.

Bill Epps - (UK) Though ex-Rhodesian Army I am also ex-RAF Regiment and I told this story at the meeting of my local East Kent branch of the RAF Regiment Association. This band who embrace campaigns from Western Europe in WWII through Suez, Cyprus, Aden, Malaya and Northern Ireland, were very impressed and moved by the dedication of the searchers and all agreed it illustrates that bond that lasts for all time between those who served together.

Norman Frodsham - 103 V.R. Squadron - What a magnificent effort by Bob and Barry. That evening, October 3rd, 1979, I was on duty at New Sarum ops room, when that dreaded news came in. I have never felt so sad and so angry at the same time. A gloom settled over the whole of Sarum. My only contribution was to be able to "field" enquiries about the whereabouts of the C.O. who was deeply emotional about our sad loss. I will always remember that evening, yet now, some 28 years later, with "pride", rather than anger or sadness. Thanks to Bob and Barry, I feel we all have a sense of closure now, knowing where our brave men gave their lives

Skatie Fourie - This must be the most gripping detail and response from our beloved countries 'madoda's and dona's' (NR expression). The finding of the Hunter. Capturing this from those in detail who were there, gives our younger generation an insight in what Rhodesia went through.

George Galbraith - SAS Regimental Association of Southern Africa - I will shortly be at the Memorial Service for our late esteemed leader and man of integrity, Mr Ian Douglas Smith. Along with him, I also salute the brave airmen who died with such honour in the sorties which have been the subject of the foregoing articles, as well as those dedicated colleagues of theirs who have brought a measure of closure to this sad event. It is both poignant and apt that, as we stand with heads bowed and hearts heavy this afternoon, we also say a special prayer for Brian, Kevin and JJ, whose proud stories also closed these many years before. God bless all our brave Rhodesian sons and daughters who have paid the price and yet make us so proud. Perhaps I should quote Rudyard Kipling's verse which he wrote for Cecil John Rhodes, for it has purchase in the stories of others who have followed like "good Old Smithie", our above friends and others :"The immense and brooding spirit still shall quicken and control, living they were the land and dead their souls shall be her soul"

Blair Gibson - I was living in Kariba at the time (Police Reserve Marine Division). We were all very upset at the time of the news that we had lost two aircraft.

Colin Graham - A Coy 10 RR Ex-Risco This magnificent find of two of our aircraft shows the determination of a certain brand of people, Rhodesians. I am so proud to have been a part of that period of time in our history. We will never forget the brave men and women of our security forces, and my children will ensure the memory survives.

Ian Graves - It's nice to hear that "Although they are gone, our comrades in arms are not forgotten" - well done.

John Hepple - I am good friends with Ivan Schafer who is Brian's uncle and lives in Port Alfred. I passed on all Bobs' news on finding the aircraft last year to Ivan.

Graham (doc) Holliday – New Zealand - Sad reading, but so glad that there has been some closure to the loss on that tragic day. I wasn't in the RRAF, but my dad was - some of you might remember him as "doctor no". Don Holliday.

Charles Holmes - Australia (4th Battalion from 1974 to 1980) - I would like to express my thanks and admiration to you and the lads who undertook the Hunter and Canberra search. It is fitting that our mates and fellow servicemen are finally laid to rest in peace.

Chris Higginson - The search for a fallen comrade is an obligation which shows respect for their sacrifice and which also shows our deep respect for their memory. How sad it is that we have not been able to carry out these duties in the way that we would have liked. The problem is not new however and I would like to mention a poem written by K.D. Clarke which is published in a book called "The Poems We Wrote" by

Eddy A Coward (Eddy lost a brother in a Lancaster during the Second World War and he produced a book which is a collection of poems that were written by aircrew that is a memorial to them all). Thank you, Bob, for all you have done to bring the memory of Brian Gordon back to us all.

Mike Huson - I had goose-bumps all over reading this article. I was tasked by AFHQ to take my Lynx and find the convoy that was being looked for by a pair of Hunters (Tony Oakley and Guy Dixon) flying low level up and down a dirt road, waiting for the OP's on the hills to tell them when they were being fired upon.

The call from AFHQ (can't remember exactly who - think it was Director Operations at the time) was a harsh ejaculation of rushed words to the effect – "Why was I not airborne? And did I realize that there were Hunters out there doing my Job - Get my Arse in the air and find the convoy that the Hunters are searching for. Call them on my way in for further references, it's on the same road that the tank was sighted on earlier that week - Get Going!"

I asked Ops to get some more info while I set off to get the Lynx prepped and dashed off to the area. I could hear Tony Oakley talking to the OP's up and down the road asking them to tell him as soon as they could hear any shooting. Tony advised the OP's that the Hunters would pitch up immediately that they were advised of any shooting so that they might be able to identify where the convoy had disappeared to. I contacted Tony and asked for their position, advised them to clear off the road and commenced flying north along the road while asking the Hunters to position to an IP and advise me their status. I remember that it was not more than 10 - 20 minutes before Tony advised that they were leaving the area and would be replaced by Brian and Ziggy.

Mike commented: "*A note at this point is that I had still not received a full briefing as to the objective of the exercise or what size of effort we were about to throw at this questionable force that was somewhere on the road. It was a surprise when the 2 Canberras arrived unexpectedly; and the pattern that they intended to fly was also in some doubt - I actually left the process of who would do what and when to the two Canberra pilots. It was an even bigger surprise to see how much flack they threw at Kevin on his final run in. This was not some small convoy with a few supporting artillery pieces. An after-thought is that we may have been set up!*"

Later, in November, I was on the receiving end of two 57AAA at night from the military base at Kafue, South of Lusaka, when we were searching for J Nkomo's supposed convoy and shortly before the Mulungushi air raid and been knocked upside down with the sound of shrapnel (sounds like a hundred cats trying to stay attached to the aircraft) screeching around the aircraft to realize what I had been lucky enough to miss in this event)

As I flew down the right side of the road at about 3-4000 feet AGL the visibility was poor from smoke and haze and the only thing that alerted me to the fact that there were un-friendlies beneath me was the eruption of flack at the same height. Closely preceding the grey clouds erupting around me were white tracer rounds and the usual red and green tracer associated with 12.7mm and 14.5mm armament. My orbit around the triangular intersection of an easterly T-junction kept me inside the maximum elevation of the ground fire. The flack was new, and the white tracer also had me wondering what down stairs was - the 3-barrel 20mm cannon - first time used in the Rhodesian War. I had found the convoy at the T-junction, where they proceeded to fire at me with various armaments.

I relayed the position to Gordon and Ziggy and received the usual responses that the target area was identified. The usual cautions were issued regarding the state of unfriendly affairs with a recommendation that they attack from the West. I seem to remember that Brian was first to attack and that during his first burst of fire hitting the ground I was already giving a correction "Add two hundred" that Brian managed to fire again and on target before pitching up out of the dive and banking to the right. The second burst hit something big, as a huge ball of black smoke enclosing a vast quantity of flames erupted from the ground. I lost sight of Brian as he was banking right behind this ball of smoke and flames.

Ziggy said that he had seen the position of the last hit (no surprises there!) and advised he was turning in live. Ziggy's attack was also in the target area and by this time the amount of flack had reduced to nothing.

After this point it went very quiet for what seemed a long time but perhaps this was because so much had been happening in a short space of time. The next radio message was Ziggy inquiring if there had been any comms from Brian. I immediately selected the emergency frequency to see if there was a PELBA signal and made a call to see if there might be some possible response. There was nothing. After a while Ziggy called in to say he was leaving the area and that he still had no comms with Brian. Almost immediately I was contacted by the lead Canberra. I once again gave the co-ordinates and description of the area. I asked for a description of their armament load and was advised that lead (?) was carrying 1000-pounders and Kevin was carrying the Alphas (bouncing balls of bad business). The Lead Canberra advised that he have to do his run in at (not sure here - but I think it was 10 000 feet) but the visibility was too poor for him to identify the target area. At this point Kevin communicated that he knew the area and was low-level and approaching from the South along the road. I asked the Lead Canberra to hold at altitude and asked Kevin to call me with the target in sight. I saw Kevin's Canberra before he called beetling up the road. The convoy was unaware of his approach as there was no flack in his direction and minimal coming up at me at this stage. Kevin let go his first load which dropped short 200 meters. I gave the correction and lost Kevin as he disappeared in to the haze on his right hand turn out.

I picked him up again to the South as he commenced the run in. This time there was a solid wall of tracer and flack about 1 - 2 km's down the road - right in Kevin's path. I advised Kevin that there was extremely heavy fire coming his way - a wall of flack at about 1 K. He responded that it was OK - shouldn't be too bad! I stressed that it looked really badly to which he responded "on the run in! There was no load dropped on that last run and the last picture I had of Kevin's Canberra was after it pitched up level with my aircraft and passed behind me to the North with about 45 plus degrees of bank on. (It turned out that the aircraft must have gone straight down in that position - that's as close as you could get to where I was and where they found the little that was left on the ground).

I advised that there had been no drop and after numerous calls there was no response from Kevin. I asked the Lead Canberra his intentions and he said that he was unable to do anything because of the conditions and was leaving the area. I advised that I remain as long as possible and continue calls and listen out.

I was called up, I think it was by one of the OP's, and advised to RTB (return to base).

On arrival - I was questioned about the losses, which was a shock really. I was a bit "bullet proof" and supposed that we all were, and to be told that two aircraft and three of our crew had gone missing was a serious blow... especially on my watch. We could not afford to lose any one of us to my mind.

I was really numb and didn't really ask too many questions or go searching for answers. Rick Culpan came to Grand Reef to do the investigation. I somehow remember that Spook Geraty was involved somewhere too. I answered more questions with Rick (Sadly Rick Culpan is no longer with us - he was killed doing aerobatics in a Provost) *at 1 Squadron on my return too.*

"I shall always remember Brian for his model aircraft - which seemed very advanced at that time and for his sense of humour - I still carry a scar on the back of my left hand as testament to his lightening

reactions with a fork to one of my childish pranks. Kevin I shall remember for his Romeo ways and devil-may-care style that was the envy of a lot of us younger officers.

Ron Janson - A closure for a very sad incident. Your perseverance and dedication to finding the site is truly admirable.

Bryan Jarman – Durban - I will never cease to be amazed with the guts and determination that Rhodesians still have today. The honour of receiving these reports and digesting them must surely be emblazed in each of us for all time. No words can express our thanks to Bob Manser, Barry Meikle, yourself and Prop and rest of the team. Well done guys.

Robert Johnson, Canada - Even after all these years I still marvel at the spirit and courage shown by the Rhodesian security forces. Your efforts to honour fallen heroes proves yet again that Rhodesians really are made of the right stuff.

Mike Jones - 1 RAR and 2RR Indonesia - Well done you guys, but one never expects anything less from the Blues.

George Killey - Great effort. I personally knew both Elliot and Brian. I was deeply saddened at the loss; and am very pleased with what you all did, bless you and a big thanks.

Günter Knieper - BSAP PATU - What a great effort. Well done

Mark (Willie) Knight – Queensland, Australia - I have been following this story with great enthusiasm. Kevin had two brothers Russell & Neville. The last I heard of them Russell was in Durban and Neville in Harare.

Bobby Knott - What a great story and closure to a very sad day to us all, if I remember correctly Seggie Seegmuller was in the other Hunter with Brian, I am very proud to have served with and on the squadron with these great Rhodesians. To Dave Bourhill I remember when you came back with that huge hole in your wing and watching you land on one main wheel with the 230 gal tank acting as the other wheel, I was at the end of the runway at the time waiting to unplug, very scary time...

Ken Kyle - Well done guys this brings back lots of memories of being on FAFs with 7 Squadron and, as a lowly Nutshell, helping as much as possible to keep them going. Even let them choose their own in-flight rations! Had quite a few dealings with Prop too as Adj. of 106 VR Sqn.

Vanessa and George Little - What a wonderful effort in true Rhodesian spirit. My husband was in the BSAP we lived and worked in Rhodesia from 1965-1979 the best years of my life and where our sons were born. A wonderful man Mr Ian Douglas Smith he now rests in peace.

David Long - I worked for many years with Brian's father, Elliot Gordon, we were both signal technicians on Rhodesia Railways and I know that Elliot spent a stint in Dete. His father and I were working in Gwelo and he was in fact visiting me at the time Brian took off on his ill-fated flight.

Simon Maitland - I must state that I am so impressed with my mate Bob Manser (15/ 16 / 17 Technical course January 1964) and his discovery of the Hunter and Canberra crash sites in Moçambique. Kevin Peinke was on my flying course 26 PTC and do miss him and my best man Keith Goddard, both who perished in that land.

Shirley Martens (nee Gordon) - On 6th November 2007, we learnt of your website from a dear friend, Mike Simpson and after some 28 years, of constant wondering about where and what happened to my beloved brother, Brian, on that fateful day of 3 October 1979 my parents, my sister and myself eventually have some form of closure and for this we thank you. You wanted to know if the Brian Gordon that your wife taught at Sir Roy Welensky school in Dett was the same person - yes it was. In fact, Brian, my sister Angela and I attended that school when we lived in Dett. I and my family would like to take this opportunity of thanking you most sincerely for what you have done and would appreciate it if we could hear from you or anyone else who knew Brian. Thanks to all concerned. So glad the past heroes have not been forgotten. Long may their memory live with us.

Gus Mason – Johannesburg - A very moving story Eddy. Thank you.

Hamish McBain - (ex-Operations Officer 101 Squadron VR) Johannesburg - Thank you to all those who still care so much and strive to preserve the memory of a dedicated and effective little Air Force. I am proud to have known Kevin Peinke from his time in 7 Squadron and

Fire Force activities. Being a small force, every loss was felt deeply by all members and the recollections published here still evoke strong feelings.

Brian McKelvin - I had a lot of contact with Kevin Peinke when he was on 7 Squadron – his callsign was 'Romeo 7' – which I thought was entirely appropriate as he had an eye for any lovely girls who were around. Kevin used to deploy with a smallish motor bike which he could use to get around with at a FAF. As Ops Officer at FAF 8 I once had to arrange to send the bike by Dakota to Kevin when the Fire Force was re-deployed to a new location!

Nic Meikle - May I say well done to the guys for their superb efforts in locating Brian Gordon's Hunter crash site. Some closure at least especially for the family. Michel (Ziggy) Seegmuller (Brian's wingman on the day) had told me of the find about 10 days ago when we bumped into each other on tour with MK. It naturally prompted reminiscing and we re-discovered as is always the case how in a small outfit like we had, how much such an event impacted (and still does) on us all. I remember the day very well having come to work on the bus and sat behind JJ Strydom; then later seeing the Canberra being called out and later again .... some very sad and unbelievable news! The previous day we (including Kev Peinke) had been down in Bulawayo

Tino Mogentale - I was an airframe tech at the time on 1 Squadron. This was one of the saddest moments of our lives waiting for Brian Gordon's return. I was the tech who dispatched the Hunters. It is forever in my head, that empty parking bay, with chocks, ladder and engine blanks waiting for the Hunter's return.

Paul Mroz – USA - I have kept my comments and thoughts to myself on this story for a while so as to let all those remarkable men that served in the RAF (Rhodesian Air Force) say their piece and "Peace", be assured, I think this left a lump in all Rhodesians throat! Fantastic, God bless, RIP all who died for Rhodesia.

Ken Palmer - To the entire team involved regarding the effort and sheer determination in researching and finding where our lost friends and colleagues made the ultimate sacrifice for Rhodesia, I can only stand by what Prop says and say I "Salute you". This is a wonderful thing to happen and finally these forever lost but not forgotten souls may now rest in peace. Having been a part of "Operation *Miracle*" this op has been in my thoughts daily since 1979. Five good men lost their lives on Op Miracle and will forever be remembered. Brian Gordon, Kevin Peinke, JJ Strydom, Gert O'Neill and Ted Mann. Gentlemen and Ladies of ORAFs if ever a Plaque is constructed with the names of these five men please let me know as I would love to donate something toward it. I think if it could be rock bolted to Monte Casino that would be a fitting gesture in their honour. Well done to all involved. "PAMWE CHETE"

Richard Palmer - A really very interesting story and as you might remember Ian Mac, Dave Shaw, Frog Ellis, Pete Buckle and I were the last Avon crew to bolt the E.R.S. doors closed.

Paul Perioli – Umhlanga Tours – Tossed a coin with JJ to decide who would fly with Kevin. Turned out I got lucky. Target acquisition at 10 000 feet was impossible. Kevin descended low-level and must have passed over the target about four times, in a left hand race-track, dropping single hoppers. Not all bombs were dropped.

Rob Pompe - I left Rhodesia in April 1979. This incident is of great significance to the whole war story. It is amazing that there is still wreckage to be found.

Jeff Rossiter, Dubai - Brian was a cadet on PTC30 at Thornhill in 1976 along with these guys: Donnelly, Jeff (me), Loftus, Scott, Dave Shirley, Henderson, Alistair Thorogood, Doug Rees, Zengerink, Guinness, Durrad, Harrington-Johnson, Kruger, Passow, Skinner, Walter, FitzGerald, McCormick, Brick Bryson, Cockcroft, Fincham, Darkes, and Charles Ashford. Brian was on a mission from day one to fly the Hunter . . . thank you for bringing us the end of his noble story.

Keith Samler - It's only a pleasure to allow you use of those pictures (in Selous Scouts) - and any others of mine you may come across. I'd like to point out a couple of things just to set the record straight. Firstly, I was not on Op Miracle, so any photographs taken there are not mine. I was on the first Chimoio raid where I took a lot of pictures and movie footage which Peter Stiff used in the first Selous Scouts book and Barbara Cole used in her SAS book "The Elite". Other pics of mine were used in a Book titled "Chimurenga" by Paul Moorcroft/Peter McLaughlin. There was some confusion in getting negatives returned from Peter Stiff after publication of "Top Secret War" and some went missing or returned to the wrong people. I think Pete Stanton will shed much lighter on the Op Miracle pictures. The picture you refer to of the AA gun undercarriage on top of Monte Casino I have not seen (I don't know which book by Peter Stiff this relates to but is certainly not mine if it was taken on Op Miracle). My pics of the AA gun were taken at Chimoio and as far as I can remember the published ones were stills extracted from the movie footage. I still have the movie footage which I had downloaded from Super 8 to VCR. There is a lot of flying on it, to and from the Chimoio raid and to and from the Mboroma and Tembue raids. I can mail it to you should you wish to see it. I hope I have been of some assistance to you. Life moves in mysterious ways and strange as it may seem I have just recently read your book about Rhodesian Air Force Operations. A really detailed and thorough account which must have required painstaking and lengthy research. I am only too pleased to assist in any small way somebody who is as meticulous and obviously takes so much pride in his work. I also read every word on the ORAFs website about the Hunter and Canberra downing. What a tremendous effort and fitting way to at last allow the crews to rest in peace.

Brad Schafer - Hello fellow Rhodesian's Zimbabwean's. This was a most intriguing story for me as an ex-serviceman (RLI and RHACR). I was a member that also took part in these raids. I was however left in the rear due to a previous injury. I read all the Rhodie stuff I can find. Hats off to those who undertake the mammoth task of documenting our past and finding the final resting place of fallen comrades. As the years go by, we the survivors grow less in numbers. The lost tribe's numbers dwindle. These stories need to be documented so we can pass them down to our children and grandchildren. It always saddens my heart to remember those great days and a great band of people. To those who paid the ultimate price you may not be known but you are never forgotten. RIP to all those who fell both in battle and in the following time of peace.

Michel (Ziggy) Seegmuller - I took great interest in the story of how you succeeded in discovering the crash site of Brian's Hunter - true perseverance indeed - well done!!! I was Brian's wingman on that dreaded 3rd October in 1979, and I have included a recounting of the events of that day out of my memoirs for your info.

Glen Seymour Hall ex BSAP - A great effort from all concerned. Our farm had been used as a base for the FAF in Penhalonga we watched this scene unfold and can only pay tribute to those who lost their lives so that we may continue. Lake Alexander holds many secrets about this operation.

Bryan Simon, Australia - Fantastic detective work. Well done for the perseverance in tracking down the site after all these years.

Gordon (Beaver) Shaw - Excellent work and it gives closure. The parts found are the compressor discs from the engine. I worked at ERS and remember the Avon engine well.

Mike Simpson, Edenvale - I can appreciate what Elliot has gone through as I lost a daughter seven years ago - Belinda was 23. I was BSAP Air Wing (PRAW) Matabeleland Province.

Diarmid Smith - Excellent article Eddy and congratulations to all concerned.

Keith Spence - As fate would have it, Kevin Peinke was not meant to be on that ill-fated air strike. Keith Spence did a re-familiarisation flight to the Range with navigator Paul Perioli on 1st October – having just returned from his honeymoon, in the UK. Sqn Ldr Ted Brent briefed Keith and his normal navigator to JJ Strydom to fly number two to Sqn Ldr Dave Rowe and Perioli for the air strike on the 3rd, but Kevin asked Keith if he could do the sortie in his stead. Ted Brent agreed to Kevin's request. The rest is now history.

Peter Stanton - I received an article via other means in respect of the two aircraft losses during Operation *Miracle*. I took part in that operation and remember the losses well. Video footage has been located of the air attack (Hunters only) on the ZANLA Chimoio complex and can be seen on the DVD accompanying the new RLI book "The Saints".

Rene Strydom – London. I was amazed when I found this site (OurStory). Thank you to all concerned that have made it possible. I am one of the daughters of JJ Strydom, and have forwarded this site to my sister Monica Palmer (Strydom), and mother; Josie Jones. Your time and effort in this project are much appreciated! Words cannot express my admiration and gratitude.

Strydom, Uysie / Josie Jones - I am the widow of JJ. I got your e-mail address through my daughter Rene. I would like to thank you and everybody that was involved in the mission last year in November. It means a lot to me and my girls to have seen the place where their Dad was killed. I feel very emotional at the moment and feel I cannot express myself in words, as this has brought back so many memories.

Jug Thornton - (Humble Brown Job) - Hong Kong - This two-part series on finding the Hunter and Canberra crash sites is humbling. What a fine effort by all involved and a great tribute to the lost crews. Fantastic! Kevin Peinke and I were good friends and well-suited as a K-Car pair. Kevin and I were both cards carrying members of "Dwarf Power". On the many Fire Force call outs I deployed on with Kevin as K-Car pilot from various FAFs, we were able to take extra ammo and max fuel loads enabling us to remain on the scene longer than most before deploying for fuel. It is sad that this discovery had to take place at all. The prayers said at the two sites was a fine ending to these stories. Well done to you and all involved in running and maintaining this great web connection. Sadly, we Brown Jobs are left only able lob insults at each other via email from time to time. All the best and thank you.

Al Thorogood - I was on helos at the time and located Kevin's crash site - we were based at Lake Alexander and I was called out when Brian went in. Unfortunately, we were unable to locate his crash site as is was on the road and the spot was a tad warm, but we did find Kevin's site which was not too pleasant.

Peter van Dyk - Well done on this achievement. It's always interesting to discover a little more about what was going on in other parts of the country. It's like a bit of jigsaw. Like most of us in the military at the time, I was too young to understand the enormity of what we were trying to accomplish. As I grow older, I appreciate it more. Recollections help.

John van Zijl (14 Trp, 3Cdo, RLI) - Thank you for the effort you made to honour our fallen. My memories of Rhodesia live with me every day.

Derek Webber (Ex Royal Air Force) - Having lived in Umtali many years ago as a teenager it is touching to read stories of a once happy thriving country when compared to today. Long may Rhodesia remain in the hearts of us all.

Chris Whitehead (Rhodesians Worldwide magazine) - Thank you to all involved-after all these years there can be some closure placed on this incident and sad loss.

Vic Wightman – UK - Mac, your efforts on the deal for a memorial to Kevin Peinke and Brian Gordon are so good. I follow that story all the way because it was such a sad time in my life losing those lovely young men.

Angie Wigmore (prev. Findlay) - Heart-warming to know that people still care enough to seek out these tragic crash sites after so many years. In 1976 I joined RBC and, sadly, was duty announcer on both occasions of the Viscount Disasters, the Hunyani and then the Umniati. If there's any consolation for the families and friends of all those lost during the war years, perhaps it's that they have not suffered the pain of the destruction of our beloved country.

Marian Wilson - Auckland New Zealand - Well done Gents. Your dedication and courage speak for itself. We do not forget our fallen heroes. I lost too many friends in Rhodesia, but each one would not have had it any different. Beloved friend Ricky. Amazing Boss John McGarrell, Canadian who Loved and Died for Rhodesia and a whole family lost in the Viscount shot down near Kariba. We were and still are one of a kind. God Bless you all, especially in this time of mourning, with the passing of Rt Hon Ian Douglas Smith. Beautifully written - thank you.

Robert Winston-Burnett - So many hero's in our great lands of once saner Rhodesia. Well done in highlighting this vital story and for sharing it with us. What a shame so many gave their everything, only for so many now to be suffering and those having their pensions stolen. We try to keep the visions alive - so please visit Humba Gushley.

Jose Zemira - Portugal - God bless all our brave Rhodesians. Our country will never die, and no matter where we are, we will... (Let our hearts beat bravely always, for this land within thy care). Well done.

Andy - Well done guys, this illustrates well the tenacity that saved many a gravel cruncher's butts. Really glad the families can get closure on this.

Clive - Pinetown - Well done guys. Now the families and loved ones can rest in peace.

Chris - I worked for Brian's father Elliot Gordon at the time Brian crashed; I remember two senior officers come to the office to inform him. At that time, I was working in land mine alley, the railway line from Gwelo to Beit Bridge.

Dave - I remember the tragic incident well. I was running the flight line on 1 Squadron in those days, although I was not on the Standby Crew that saw the aircraft off on that day. So, I only learned about the Hunter R1821 crash the following morning. I have many happy memories of my 12 years on 1 Squadron, but Brian Gordon's loss was the most tragic low point of it all.

Doug S - Zimbabwe - Amazing, we were men amongst men.

Earl (Sconny Don?**) -** Rhodesians Never Die. Although we are the last of a generation. Keep up the spirit wherever you may be.

George - It is only when one's mind is taken back to those days by stories like this that the reality sinks in as to just what a fine bunch of guys, we had around us in those days compared to the average people we now associate with, wherever we are scattered around the world.

Graham (ex A.S.F. New Sarum) - Well done guys. We had all been drinking at Lake Mac in Kevin's boat house the week before he crashed. I can also remember when Kevin did a low-level fly past at the lake one afternoon on his return from a flight (low meaning the water in lake Mac rippled - less than 100 feet!!!).

Howard (BSAP and PATU) - Great work to all involved. I was Involved in many incidents where we relied on the Rhodesian Air Force for backup. They were always there no matter how limited their resources or how dangerous the task. Rhodesian Never Die!!!

John - Well Done, So many brave Rhodesians need to be remembered, your discovery does a lot towards those memories.

John – New Zealand - It is wonderful that so many have that eternal fire in their veins and have gone to great lengths to follow up on their comrades and to pay respect after so many years. The way the comments have unfolded it sounds like this only took place yesterday, the memories are still crystal clear and leave us with a lump in our throats. Thanks to the dedicated efforts of Bob and Barry and others in travelling through hostile terrain to confirm the Hunter and Canberra sites.

John – Also New Zealand. There were so few of us to face the rest of the world. I thank one and all for keeping the home fires and memories warm in our hearts. "We shall remember them . . . . . "

Tony Canada - Thank you very much for taking the time to record this event for history.

Ken (ex RAF) - Hi. My wife was in Rhodesia from 1974 and left in 1979 and had some wonderful tales to tell. Your stories were wonderful; some left a lump in my throat. I will keep in touch.

Ken - What can I say but that Rhodesians are one of a kind. Thanks to all concerned that has made it possible for the families of these men to finally have closure. It is truly remarkable that even though we Rhodesians are spread around this world, we can still unite and form that unbreakable bond on matters that concern our people. These men are our heroes and will never be forgotten. Pamwe Chete.

Nick - Well done Bob & Barry on your perseverance in finding the site. I [like Ken] am also willing to contribute towards a plaque in honour of these Brave Men who made the ultimate sacrifice for their people and country.

Owen - Men like Brian and Kevin are few and far between. What a tragic loss, especially made sadder when the ruin of Rhodesia stares at us in the headlines every day ....No one can doubt that the Rhodesians were right. Rest peacefully guys.

Peter - I was in the RLI at the time but not involved in the Operation. But I always appreciate those who take the time to go back in time and research events that happened many years ago. I remember hearing about the downed aircraft and was shocked that it could happen to 'us' as I believed we were invincible. Time was to prove us wrong, but we all did our best under difficult conditions.

Robert - I was in Umtali when this tragedy was unfolding, I remember 2 Hunters flying over the city. Brian was a very pleasant and easy-going gentleman, the occasional ride back to Thornhill on his bike, and at times along the railway line was common after a few too many at the Midlands Hotel. I do remember one occasion when a number of Hunters were flying towards the flight line from the direction of the tower, and we airmen were standing watching from under the trees at 1 Squadron, Boss Vic Wightman was leading, and Brian was taking up the rear of the flight. Boss Wightman calmly said over the radio " Mr Gordon would you please catch up". Brian was flying at the rear, but also had the lowest position in the formation and a beat up was possible. After landing Brian mentioned that he was hoping the "Boss" wouldn't notice how low the rear man was, a big grin on his face. A Gentleman that we have lost but never forgotten.

Fly Forever Brian The Sky has no limit for you.

Roger - As a former member of the BSAP/CIO, I've always had a great admiration for all members of the RRAF. This recent Moçambique venture to locate the site of impact of both the missing Hunter and Canberra brings a suitable closure on the demise these brave men. May they now rest in peace.

Steve - I observed on a number of occasions Hunter strikes on terr positions the most memorable of which had to be at Monte Casino. We had just cleared and neutralised a trench system and had a few moments to watch the Hunters performing a strike on the "Rock" which was Monte Casino. They had to run the gauntlet of enemy fire which included 38mm cannon flak, 14,5 mm AA Guns and the newest 20mm 3 barrelled Hotchkiss AA Gun (interestingly, we found the 20mm Hotchkiss buried in a maize munda after the event - Ron Reid-Daly / Peter Stiff claimed thirty seven millimetre gun positions were found abandoned). The courage and sheer determination shown by both Air Force and ground forces during that engagement will forever be branded in my mind. Sadly, we lost Gert O'Neill and Ted Mann. We, the living, will forever remember and honour those who fell at Monte Casino.

Stuart - What a great effort. Well done.

Terry - Port Elizabeth - I felt all those wonderful emotions that we keep locked away after losing a close friend, all come flooding back when I read these articles. What friends these men must have been. Thanks for allowing me to share your emotions.

Tony – Canada - Thank you very much for taking the time to record this event for history.

Vic Australia - What a fantastic effort, well done.

Rick van Malsen writes:- The story on the search for the two aircraft lost post Op Miracle brought back a few memories as 1 Commando RLI were very involved in this second phase of the operation.

I concluded: "With respectful thanks to James 'Tackie' Bannerman for pasting the maps together, and marking the sites where Kevin Peinke's Canberra and Brian Gordon's Hunter went down on the

3rd October 1979, this Chapter to our downed crews is now complete. We now know for a fact the exact spot where our Air Force colleagues were so honourably killed in action.

"Bob Manser has given much credit to Barry Meikle (and justifiably so) in locating the Canberra remains, this in no small measure detracts from Bob's original stated intention right at the onset of these phenomenal expeditions to find his mate Kevin's final resting place (and of course, Brian's as well).

"I am not ashamed to admit the deep emotional impression it made on me to read Bob's "fact-story', and also being privileged to be one of the first to absorb the many photographs Bob sent Eddy Norris and I. The Hunter find came just too late for inclusion in my *Operations Book*, but with Bobs permission I wish to include most of them in an abridged version of my *Nickel Cross* - which I am now motivated to follow as a supplement to the Operations book. I have headed the chapter by what I consider a most appropriate and moving 'Once was Lost, But now am Found' heading."

Once was Lost - But now am Found
Killed in Action – 3 October 1979

Air Lieutenant Brian Kevin Gordon   No 1 Squadron
Flight Lieutenant Kevin Leslie Peinke No 5 Squadron
Flight Lieutenant Johannes Jacobus Strydom No 5 Squadron

ONCE WAS LOST BUT NOW AM FOUND

Finding the Hunter
 http://www.ourstory.com/thread.html?t=290507#296121

WRECKAGE

Bob Manser recovered a wrecked starter and a small piece of bone-dome from the Canberra crash site, and a couple of 30mm doppies from the Hunter crash site – and shipped the bits from Chimoio down to Durban where they were uplifted by Kutanga John McKenzie. Kutanga Mac, by now well known for his special brand of 'Medals Presentations', set out to sculpture a fitting memorial as an everlasting token to honour our fallen comrades. Big Mac alerted the world to this plight in a despatch titled the Ombudsman. Despite receiving mixed messages in return, the decision was taken to go ahead and fashion a suitable memorial. Eddy

Norris kindly sent out word via ORAFs and within a relatively short time responses were received from most welcome quarters. Air Vice Marshal Len Pink donated his 5 Squadron plaque, which Tol Janeke kindly fetched from Australia. Then Eddy Wilkinson sent in his 1 Squadron plaque from Cape Town, and Barry Roberts donated the centrepiece – a very hard to come by bone-dome!

HUNTER COMPRESSOR / TURBINE RECOVERY

Just as the finishing touches were made to the memorial, Bob Manser had managed to recover Brian Gordon's turbine remains from Cruzamento! His verbatim report 16 May 2008 read as follows:

"Busy morning for Pedro and me but success and coming your way soon the battered remains of a Hunter turbine. This means Kutanga Mac will have more bits to play with. No photos as we had to sneak in as unobtrusively as possible and get the turbine without arousing the locals' interest. We had to check in with the "chef de poste" the local DC and after 15 minutes with him we got permission to go and get it via the local village administrator then the local chief. Luckily, we only had to part with a few bucks here and there and we encountered no drunks as before thank goodness. We zipped in with a couple of locals, loaded up and sped out before any problems arose or anybody woke up as to what we were doing."

"So not really any time for photos as we did not want to make a 'scene' of it all. I have a couple of shots of the turbine remains on the back of my pick up and shows me trying to cut the turbine in half so making it manageable for my transporters to get it down to Jhb. Hope Kutanga Mac is able to do something with it, better it is in safe and respected resting place than left amongst the weeds in the bush".

The photo above shows the remains of the Hunter engine, as found by Bob Manser. This next photograph shows what was left of the Hunter compressor and turbine – as recovered by Bob from Cruzamento Village – and after having given it a good pressure clean. If one looks carefully at the last three rings, several twisted and wrecked blades will be noted. Another very important observation is the angle at which the rings are bent in relation to the drive-shaft.

The second photograph shows Bob kneeling on the back of the bakkie and separating two pieces, cutting with an angle grinder – in order to dispatch the engine remains from Chimoio to Benoni, and then on to Durban and Mbabane.

Prop's Brass Hunter – used for the Miracle Memorial

Remains of Hunter Avon engine

Bob Manser , with Angle Grinder, cutting the compressor

Kutanga Mac and Johnny Green, at the Shamwari Arms, deciding where to place the Op Miracle Memorial. Note the Rhodesian camouflaged bone-dome – and the inscription on the visor, which is shown more clearly elsewhere

Prop & Rina Geldenhuys, John & June McKenzie, Anne & Tol Janeke
Kutanga Mac's "steering committee"

This starter off the Canberra Avon engine was recovered by Bob Manser in November 2007.

John McKenzie 'seized' it, cleaned it, had it sand-blasted and used it on the Operation Miracle Memorial

MIRACLE MEMORIAL

Kutanga McKenzie fashioned the Operation Miracle Memorial with inspiration that can only be described as "from above". Like any admirer of a masterpiece, interpretation will come from the beholder. It is thus that there may be those who may query the 'Dove/Holy Spirit' figurine positioned above the camouflaged bone-dome. It basically represents placing God first – above all else whatever is said or done. However, to aid those who may not appreciate fully the composition of the memorial, John had this to say:

"While the writing of Prop Geldenhuys' book titled '*Rhodesian Air Force Operations with Air Strike Log*' was being recorded and correct information gathered Prop and I pondered on the circumstances, facts or condition connected with the aftermath, the consequences of an unpleasant event during Operation Miracle concerning the Air Force losses of aircrew and aircraft. We found ourselves at a loss as there were no answer to this dilemma other, then register downed aircraft and aircrew killed in action. Our spirits grieved such that we were led to pray forgiveness on behalf of our nation's folly and foolishness. During the course of repentance and led by the Holy Spirit I was inspired to dedicate a memorial in honour to our aircrew a Hunter pilot, a Canberra pilot and his navigator killed in action during Operation *Miracle*. Prop agreed and to-day we unveil that desire and the presentation here in Durban. The memorial plaque its purpose is not about religion but rather about the Holy Spirit raising up men with a dream and to commemorate and honour the memory of those killed during Operation *Miracle*.

"The plaque is made of Rhodesian railway sleeper wood, the finest of all hardwoods worldwide, its beauty depicts the strength ambitiously established and found in Rhodesians.

"Working from top of the plaque to bottom: The first image represents the Holy Spirit which by God inspired intervention I call the 'ombudsman', overseer to the whole project. Next the memorial projects a pilot's bone-dome (crash helmet) his headdress gloriously veiled in the Rhodesian camouflage, the national Battle Colours these men of valour. The helmets visor ray-ban like cut the glare to-day gleams the quality of emotion felt at war. Squadron crest a distinctive heraldic design of Speed and Courage; Seek and Destroy, protect Rhodesia, supreme sacrifice, the squadrons last call, Operation *Miracle* saved the lives of many, many more. Finally, below the squadron badges a One squadron Hunter; and Five squadron Canberra aircraft grace their pilot and navigator roll-call. Air Lieutenant, Brian Kevin Gordon of No 1 Squadron, Flight Lieutenant, Kevin Leslie Peinke, navigator Flight Lieutenant Johannes Jacobus Strydom the No 5 Squadron aircrew.

"Moving to the reverse side of the memorial we read great oracles, the love poem aviators of great mandate their flying machine. Debris recovered from the crash-site during the prayers service lace this end and final closure to the dedication memorial of Operation *Miracle* and lost aircrew.

"This memorial of such beauty, a presentation of many parts or articles I call facets relating to the operation and its consequences of valour and victory could only have been made with, as a fine and treasured monument by those declared as men with a dream of which I catalogue in no particular order - AVM Len Pink; Barry Roberts; Eddy Wilkinson; Bob Manser; Gary Albyn; Craig Fourie & Kutanga Mac

Op Miracle steering committee - Gp Capt Tol & Anne Janeke; Prop & Rina Geldenhuys & John & June McKenzie

Valuable help-line -Gorg and Kurtis van der Linde; Victor Irwin & Shanil Sardeo".

Should Graham Patterson and Ken Palmer read this, they will get a great sense of satisfaction when readers take note that they were one of the first to commit towards the ideal of some sort of memorial, like Johns', which is now a reality.

We are also particularly pleased to have made contact with all the next-of kin, all of whom have indicated that they would be attending the Re-union on the 29th anniversary date and would be present at the Unveiling of the Memorial.

Firstly, Brian's parents Elliot and Rita Gordon from Sedgefield, JJ Stardom's widow Josie Jones from Pietermaritzburg and Kevin's brother Russell Peinke from Umdloti. Our thoughts and prayers will be with those relatives who are overseas or just too distant – like flying in from London being out of the question. However, our thoughts will be with JJ's daughters Rene and, and Kevin's eldest brother Neville in Harare.

We also wish to acknowledge those folk who have said they will gather on the 3rd October 2008 – being Gary Albyn, Terry Bennett, Roland and Wendy Charles, Brett and Dina Charles, Trish d'Hotman, Chris and Margaret Dams, Pey and Eloise Geldenhuys, Elliot and Rita Gordon, Angela and daughter Christine, Johnny and Noeleen Green, Ivan Holtshauzen, Toll and Anne Janeke, Sonny and Caroline Janeke, Bob Manser, Shirley Martens and partner Pat, Brian McKelvin, John and June McKenzie, Russell and Cynthia Peinke, Paul Perioli and Gerta, Barry Roberts, Ivan and Lenore Schafer, Mike Simpson, Dave and Joan Stone, Kurtis and Gorg van der Linde, Boet van Schalkwyk, and Pete and Ellie Woolcock.

MIRACLE MEMORIAL HAWKER HUNTER

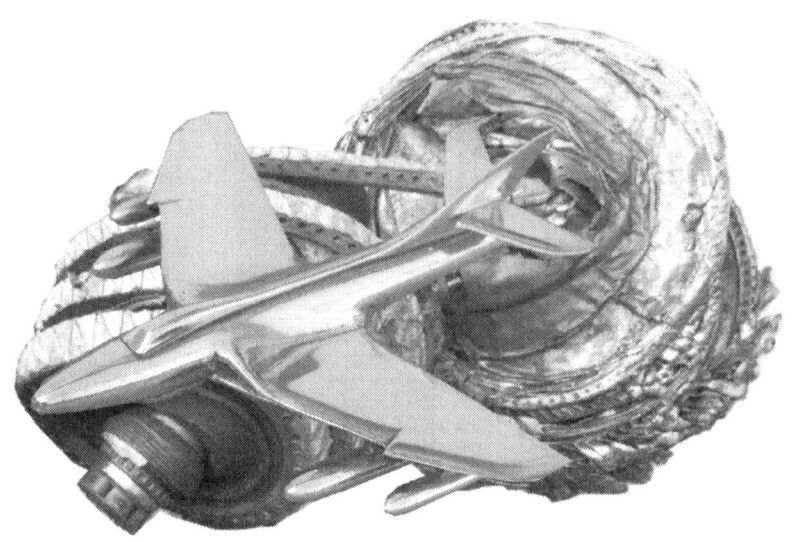

FRELIMO WAR MUSEUM – MAPUTO

John McKenzie and I had hoped to visit Maputo to see what we could unearth regarding FRELIMO records relevant to Operation *Miracle*. This was planned with some trepidation, as some readers may appreciate the authorities would not naturally welcome previous combatants with open arms. However, the driving force all along had been to establish what exactly happened to the Rhodesian aircrews twenty-nine years ago – and to establish where the remains were buried. This surely, is the burning question at the back of the minds of everyone who has had knowledge of Operation *Miracle*.

Unfortunately, our trip to Maputo was called off a mere week before departure, because the FRELIMO War museum Museu da Revolução was closed to the general public due to renovations taking place – or "Rehabilitation till January" as the Director, Adriano Mariquele replied when I asked. When Adriano agreed to see us, we wasted no time getting to Maputo. Admittedly, some sweet talking was necessary to get the written "Solicitação de Bons Ofícios" acceptable to the Moçambique History Archives (Arqivo Histórico de Moçambique). Adriano did us proud and found most of what we wanted by calling for the Noticias newspaper reports spanning the years 1977 and 1979.

Letter from FRELIMO addressed to History Archives of Moçambique

This was but one of many obstacles that was faced in meeting tight deadlines. Whilst the full story is still incomplete, many readers anger will be rekindled while just as many will experience deep emotional moments as they peruse this account. I am not ashamed to admit both spectrums – moments where the folly of temperament or gung-ho boldness has cost lives and at the same time where tears of sadness has cleansed my soul. May you, also, experienced both as you near the end of this novel.

Accordingly, John and I decided that we would consider an update, after the launch, should demand warrant it. Bob, in all likelihood, would also have found the Donaldson Canberra near Malvernia by then? Being true to his word, and knowing Bob, he just won't rest until this ambition has been realised. I won't be at all surprised to hear the next Stop Press statement from him "Manser and Brendon Bekker find Operation *Manyatela* Canberra, which was lost near Malvernia"! Another once was lost but now am found tear jerker. If not yours, then mine.

Captured communist supplied weaponry and stores following an earlier Rhodesian raid on Chimoio
Photo Credit: Selous Scouts - A Pictorial Account. Peter Stiff 1984

Wheeled 12.7mm

14.5mm ZPU-4 KPV gun

Soviet Anti-Aircraft weapons captured, having been used against Lynx, Canberra and Hunter attacks

Photo: Selous Scouts, Peter Stiff

A rare photo – Our Hunter, with Sidewinder and SAAF roundel- with thanks to Eddy Norris, ORAFs and Tony Mogentale -

Op Miracle
Anti-Aircraft guns, gun pits, trenches, and ammunition boxes abandoned by ZANLA.

Photo credit - Selous Scouts
A Pictorial Account
Peter Stiff - 1983. Also
Winds of Destruction

Russian T-55 Tank

**These are Iranian Twin 35mm Cannons – not unlike
some of the Soviet supplied anti-aircraft weaponry to
FRELIMO and ZANLA**

Mini-Miracle Re-union - July 2008

Prop Geldenhuys, Josie Jones (JJ's widow), Russell Peinke & John 'Kutanga' McKenzie

KUTANGA MAC PARKED IN FRONT OF THE BARRICADED MUSEUM IN MAPUTO

Kutanga Mac charming Adriano F. Mariquele to obtain a 'Solicitacao de Bons Oficios' to the Arquivo Historico de Mocambique

These FPLM gunners claimed to have shot down the Canberra (Noticias newspaper report dated 14 October 1979)

Typical FPLM / FRELIMO Gun Batteries

Frelimo gun batteries

Maputo Museum anti-aircraft weapons display

12.7mm and 7.62mm Anti-Aircraft weapons displayed at the Revolutionary Museum

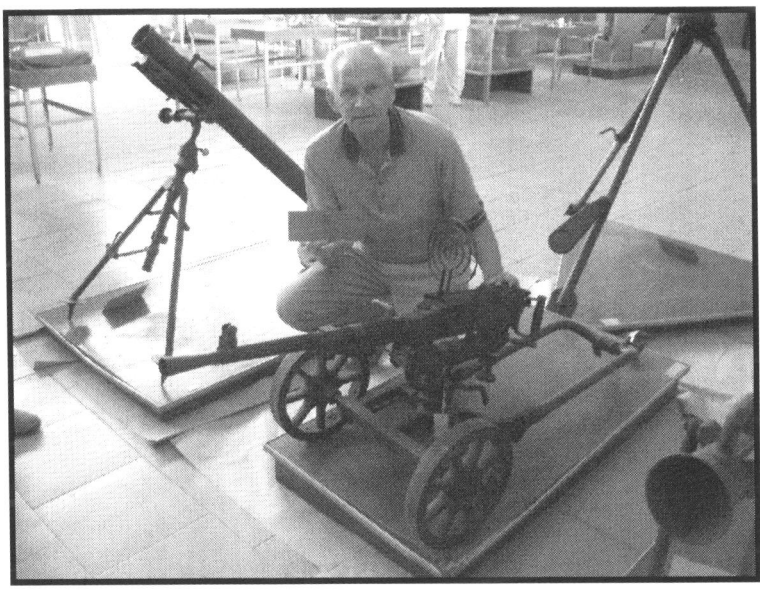

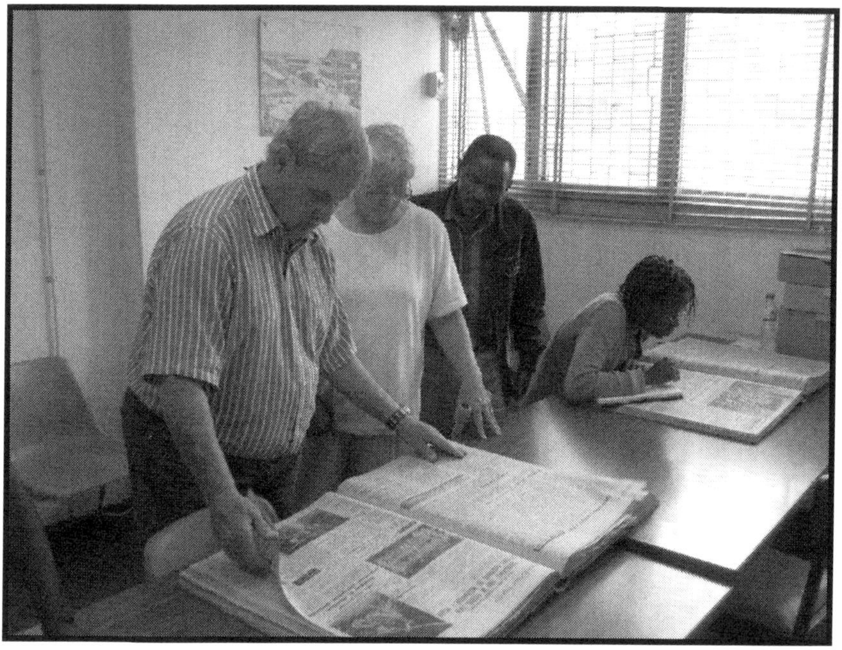

John McKenzie, Rina Geldenhuys and Adriano Mariquele researching Archive reports

nacional

AGRESSORES RODESIANOS SOFRERAM MAIOR DERROTA DE SEMPRE

• Seis aviões abatidos e mais de 120 soldados mortos
• Inimigo não conseguiu alcançar nenhum dos seus objectivos

News report in the Noticias paper, dated 14 October 1979. Hunter wreckage displayed, with gun crew claiming the Canberra

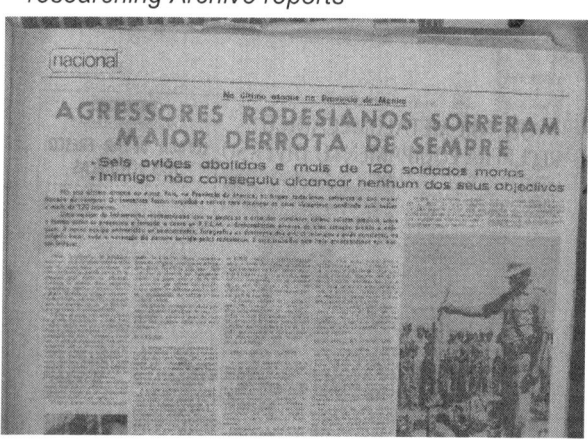

Headline reads "Rhodesian troops suffered their biggest defeat ever in their last aggression in the province of Manica, having lost six lives. About 120 men having not reached their objective. In the photo wreckage of the shot down planes report on page 3. One of the pieces used by FPLM in the bombardment of enemy positions".

Noticias Nacional press report 14 Oct 1979

The Frelimo soldier in the top right-hand picture is holding up
Brian Gordon's Hunter oleo leg and wheel hub.

The author meeting Frelimo Lieutenant-General Antonio Hama Thay
in Maputo, July 2010

*Presenting the Director of Mozambique National Archives, Prof Dr
Joel Das Neves Tempe with a copy Rhodesian Memorials*

Eduardo Mondlane historical archives

Dr Joel opened many doors for us during our searches in Mozambique. He introduced us to the Mapai Brigade Commander who unfortunately required a large some of money to 'speak freely' – he also required payment to be photographed. However, I managed to sneak one before it became too dark when night fell.

Canberra wreckage displayed – as per Moçambique Archives

A unique Rhodesian camouflaged 'Operation Miracle' bone-dome by John 'Kutanga Mac' McKenzie

The aircrew name-tags are being engraved and were not ready in time to be added with this unique camouflaged bone-dome. In the interim, full credit is given to Gorg van der Linde for the excellent job she did in covering the bone-dome, and John's artwork on the visor.

To 'match' John's artwork, but in a literary sense, I elected to insert the AIRMANS GRACE, which I trust will be used at the Unveiling:

Lord of thunderhead and Sky,
Who placed in man the will to fly
You taught his hand speed, skill and grace
To soar beyond man's dwelling place.

You shared with him the eagle's view
The right to fly as eagles do
The right to call the clouds his home
And grateful through Your heavens roam.

May we assemble here tonight
And all who love the thrill of flight
Recall with two-fold gratitude
Your gift of wings. Your gift of food.

As provided by Ian Haggie

POSTHUMOUS AWARDED KGCV

There is the right time to announce the posthumous award of the KutangaMac Grand Cross of Valour to:

Mr. Elliot Gordon – the father of Brian

Russell Peinke – the brother of Kevin

Uysie Jones – the widow of JJ Strydom

The Citations will only be made public at the Awards Ceremony, to be held on the 29th Anniversary of the loss of three very bold, brave airmen who paid the supreme sacrifice to qualify for this, the highest and most prestigious award of all the famous Kutanga Medals. The Crosses were meant to be cast from the remains of the Avon Compressor / Turbine that powered the Hunter and Canberra crews to their doom. May the dependants of these fine airmen cherish, always, the significance and meaning of these specific KGCV's.

OPERATION MIRACLE MEMORIAL UNVEILING / SERVICE

Operation *Miracle* produced another Miracle 28 years later, when our living heroes Bob Manser and Barry Meikle found the remains of Rhodesians in Moçambique – November 2007. Bob and Barry placed crosses next to the Canberra and Hunter turbine remnants.

Crosses at Crash Sites

Amazing Grace piped

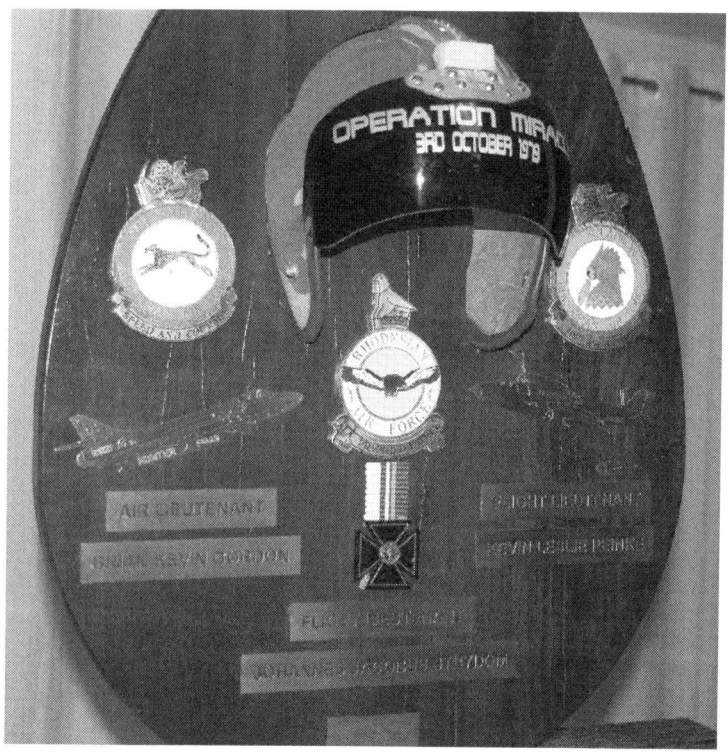

Group Captain Tol Janeke with Brian's parents Rita and Elliot

Rita and Elliot Gordon

Air Force Padre Boet van Skalkwyk

The back of the Memorial

The front with expended 30mm cannon cases

The Gordon family – Elliot, Angela, Rita and Shirley
Brian's two sisters, Shirley Martens and Angela van der Burgh were
present with the Unveiling of the Memorial.

With **not** much edging by Kutanga McKenzie, it was decided to launch the commemorative booklet at the Unveiling, on the 3rd October

2008, (which is the 29th Anniversary), at the Shamwari Club in Westville, Durban. Boet van Schalkwyk, who needs no introduction to his Air Force colleagues, kindly agreed to carry out the Votum at the Unveiling ceremony – to give the Blessing to a worthy cause. Air Vice Marshal (retired) Chris Dams had planned to unveil the memorial but on doctors' advice wisely decided not to subject Margaret to a long trip so soon after a back operation. Tol Janeke kindly stepped into the breech to perform the solemn duty of formally unveiling the Memorial. His introduction, at the beginning of the book, I believe, is the perfect speech for the Unveiling.

The Eddy Norris ORAFs condolences poem is very appropriate:

You can shed tears that they have gone
or you can smile because they had lived.

You can close your eyes and pray that they'll come back
or you can open your eyes and see all they've left.

Your heart can be empty because you can't see them
or you can be full of the love you shared.

You can turn your back on tomorrow and live yesterday
or you can be happy for tomorrow because of yesterday.

You can remember them and only that they're gone
or you can cherish their memory and let it live on.

You can cry and close your mind, be empty and turn your back
or you can do what they'd want:
smile, open your eyes, love and go on.

140

At the going down of the sun, and in the morning, We will remember gallant Brian Gordon, Kevin Peinke and J J Strydom

Operation Miracle Memorial Service

Operation Miracle Memorial – Unveiled on the 29th Anniversary on 3rd October 2008. Memorial was made by John McKenzie, and Unveiled by Tol and Anne Janeke. Dedicated to Air Lieutenant Brian Kelvin Gordon (Hunter pilot), Flight Lieutenants Kevin Peinke (Canberra pilot) and Johannes Jacobus Strydom (SAAF navigator), killed in

action,   3 October 1979. This page is dedicated to John Kutanga Mac who died 20 July 2010

Operation Miracle Memorial - Shamwari Club display – Memorials and Memorabilia

Back of the Memorial – Not shown in the photograph is the Brass Hawker Hunter FGA 9, mounted on the actual compressor ring disc recovered from the Brian Gordon crash site by Bob Manser (John Kutanga Mac McKenzie was called to higher service in July 2009)

New Farm list some 1055 ZANLA casualties – the twelve columns show about 79 names each and the last two 56 and 51 respectively.

The nine mass-graves at New Farm, Moçambique – as photographed by Bob Manser. The Zimbabwe Museums and Monuments are presently preparing exhibits for a building, situated some distance from the treed area as shown in the photograph on the preceding page.

New Farm - Liberation Struggle Shrine / Museum

L .	MANONGERO	JOHNATHAN
L .	CHITURI	K . CHITSIKU
J .	CHIKWARAKWARA	K . N. MUCHAGEZA
J .	CHIRENJE	L . MARASENI
J .	CHISAMBA	L . L. MATIKINYIDZE
J .	MANDIPERA	LAWRENCE
J .	TIYAZI	L . ZHARANDE
J .	ZINYAMA	L . DHOWERA
J .	MARIWO	L . T. NYAKABAU
J .	MATIMATI	L . F. SAMUPINDI
J . M.	ELIAS	L . N. SAMUSHONGA
J . N.	MWANAKA	L . T. DAFE
J .	ZIMUNYA	L . MANGARIRWA
J .	CHISAINYERWA	L . SIMBAI
J .	MACHOKOTO	L . MABHIZA
	LAWRENCE	LYDIA
L .	NYAMUNARO	MAGGIE

Bob Manser submitted a large number of photographs taken at the soon to be opened New Farm Museum which the Director of National Museums and Monuments, Zimbabwe had mentioned.

Bob returned to the New Farm shrine to take close-up photographs of all the names for the author. It seems at first glance that several names are duplicated, for instance Elias, Jonathan and Lawrence.

Rusted pistols

New Farm relics

The museum building is under construction as at September 2009 (32 years after Operation Dingo) – with Bob writing "the memorial site at New Farm is a rebuild of the old farm HQ. You can see some of the old weapons and also the floor and bits of wall that are pitted with shrapnel. You can see the new building bricks and new roof that they have put on over the remains of the old walls."

The remains of a Chinese 12.7mm anti-aircraft machine gun, a couple of FN rifles and 9mm pistols, with numerous and varied rifle barrels still need to be mounted and displayed.

Extract from "Rhodesian War Casualties and Air Force Memorials, published 2009 by John Dovey of Just Done Productions Publishing, Durban and subsequently printed by Lulu.com and Amazon Kindle by Peysfoft Publishing, Paeroa, New Zealand

Gordon, Brian Kevin, 4397, Air Lieutenant, Rhodesian Air Force, killed on active service, by ground fire during Operation Miracle in Moçambique, while flying a Hunter FGA9, 3 October 1979.

Operation - Miracle; Location - Cruzamento, Moçambique; Aircraft -

Hawker Hunter R 1821; Burial Site - Body not recovered

The Operation Miracle Memorial dedicated to the above three Bold Airmen was made by John "Kutanga" McKenzie, and was Unveiled by Group Captain Tol Janeke at the Shamwari Club in Westville on the 2008 Anniversary date. Operation Miracle, and the Memorial, is re-visited later on. The crash site was found by Bob Manser in November 2007.

Miracle Memorial

The Miracle Memorial is encased in a glass cabinet made by Rob Rix of Woodtime, Pinetown. The memorial features extensively elsewhere and thus the photograph below show Rob's handiwork.

Brian Gordon Memorial

This is how the Operation Miracle Memorial was displayed prior to its removal from the Shamwari/German Club in Westport, Durban – for storage at the Natal Mounted Rifles due north of the city.

AIR LIEUTENANT

BRIAN KEVIN GORDON

Bob Manser did place a white cross at the Hunter crash site at Cruzamento where Brian Gordon was killed in action. Because the village was growing rapidly with construction of pole and dagga huts, the cross was brought to the Shamwari Club, Durban. It was handed to his mother, Rita Gordon for sentimental value. The Club now houses the Operation Miracle Memorial, a more permanent home to honour the fallen.

The cross made by Bob Manser and the wreath laid by Elliot and Rita Gordon

The wreath that Elliot and Rita Gordon laid with the unveiling in October 2008 is reproduced for the record.

It will be noted that Brian shares the Memorial with the Canberra crews killed in action – Kevin Peinke and Johannes Jacobus Strydom.

Brian's Hunter turbine disc's that were sandblasted by Johnny Green at the Shamwari Club, Westville, was subsequently flogged by Mounted Rifle soldiers to scrap metal dealers.

OP MIRACLE-HUNTER FGA9
R1821 COMPRESSOR DISC-
SHOT DOWN CRUZAMENTO, MOZ
BRIAN GORDON KIA 3 OCT 1979

Hawker Hunter compressor rings on display at the Shamwari Club in Westville

Sadly – This relic of Brian's Hunter is no more. Natal Mounted Rifle's culprits seized an opportunity to 'scale' this piece of precious metal and flog it to Durban scrap-metal dealers for a few bucks. The German Club in Westport had requested the Air Force, Rhodesian Army and BSAP to remove the RSF museum exhibits from their club, which they found offended some of their members. Alternate accommodation was found at the NMR Club where the exhibits were placed in temporary storage.

Subsequent follow-up revealed the sad truth as to what happened to the 'missing' compressor disc. Well, that is sadly a fact of African life in the country.

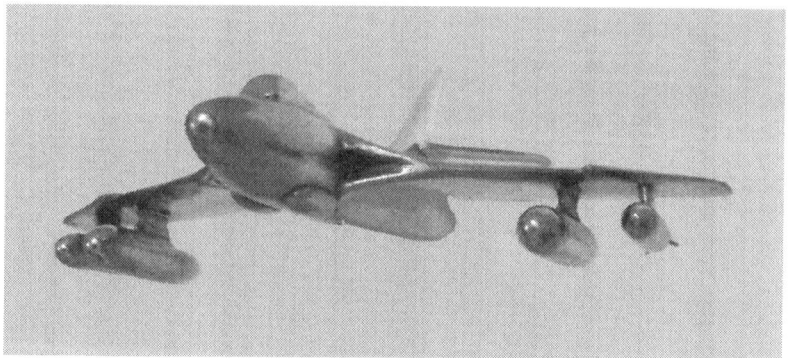

Rhodesia at war 1965 – 80 map

ACKNOWLEDGEMENTS

The author is grateful, and acknowledge, the contributions made by the following persons and organizations: -

Air Marshal Norman Walsh – retired Commander
Air Vice Marshal Chris Dams – readily supporting the project
Air Vice Marshal Len Pink – No 5 Squadron Plaque
Gary Albyn – Poetry
Tackie Bannerman – Cruzamento maps / information
Matthew Blackley - Poetry
Jason Connell – Graphic designer
Copy Shop – photo enhancements and enlargements
Guy Dixon - Hunter pilot
John Dovey – Just Done Productions Publishing / graphic artist
Craig Fourie – donating the camouflaged material
Johnny Green – Shamwari Arms go-between / Air Force display
Elliot and Rita Gordon – Brian's parents
Mike Huson – eye witness account (Lynx pilot)
Tol Janeke – Unveiling the Memorial and writing the Introduction
Pete Kloppers – Copy Shop resources and draft copies
Willie Knight – for locating Russell and Neville Peinke
Adriano Mariquele - Museu da Revolução / Arquivo Histórico
Barry Meikle – who helped Bob re-discover the crash sites
Eddy Norris – ORAFs, OurStory and Pride of Turkeys
Peter Petter-Bowyer – essential inputs, photographs and corrections
Richard Quinell – driving Bob to Cruzamento and picking up the turbine
Cas Rademaker – Transporting turbine Chimoio to Johannesburg
Barry Roberts – Bone-dome
Riana Roets – Graphic Artist
Ziggy Seegmuller - Hunter wingman
Shamwari Club Management – Memorial venue & Club facilities
Peter Stiff – for referring the authors to ex-BSAP Supt Keith Samler
Pedro Swanepoel – driving Bob and Barry and finding the Hunter site
Kevin Tidy – Flights over Monte Casino and Chimoio memorial photo
Gorg & Kurtis van der Linde - camouflaged covering of the Bone-dome
Padre Boet van Schalkwyk - Votum
Gavin Wehburg – first photographs of the Canberra crash site
Eddy Wilkinson – No 1 Squadron Plaque

And last but not least – our faithful and supportive wives and families.

Finally – a special word of thanks to Bob Manser for finding the Hunter and Canberra crash sites and the late John 'Kutanga' McKenzie for making the memorable Miracle Memorial possible. Also, already mentioned, the late Eddy Norris, the founder of ORAFs – Old Rhodesian Air Force sods.

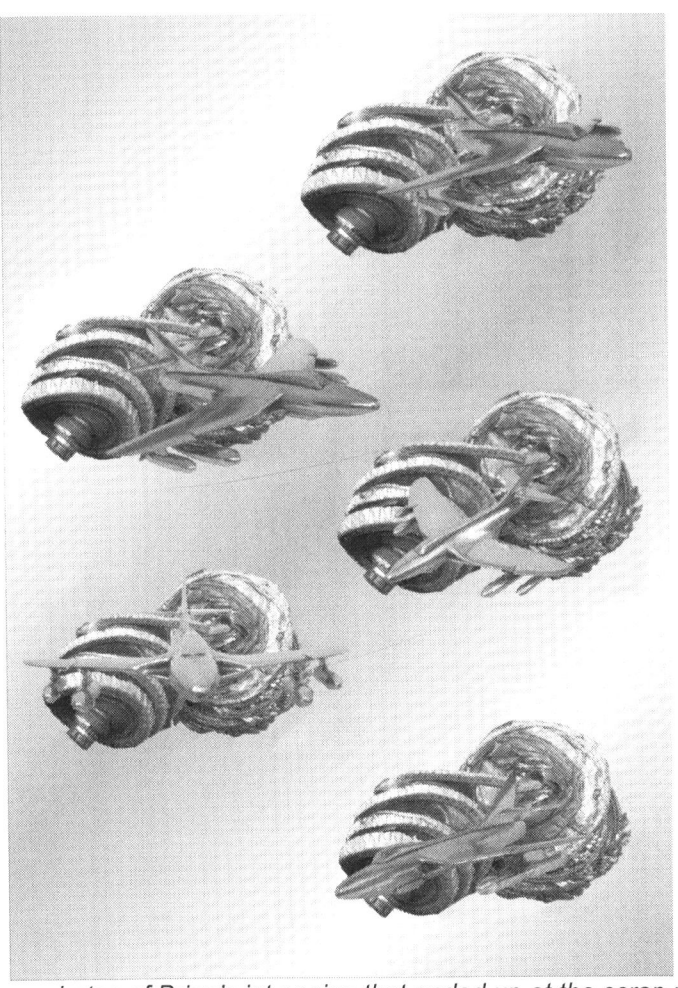

Various photos of Brian's jet engine that ended up at the scrap metal dealers (after being scaled by NMR soldiers.

153

BIBLIOGRAPHY

Nickel Cross, Just Done, 2007
Rhodesian Air Force Operations with Air Strike Log, 2007
Rhodesia-Zimbabwe Roll of Honour: War Casualties 1965 – 1980
The 38
Michael Hamence and Winston Brent, *Canberra*, Freeworld
  Publications, 1998
Noticias newspaper reports
Barry Jones, *Hawker Hunter*, Crowwood Press, 1998
Peter Petter-Bowyer, *Winds of Destruction*, Trafford, 2003
Peter Stiff, *Selous Scouts*, Galago, 1984

Other Books by the same Author

Rhodesian Air Force Operations
Rhodesia-Zimbabwe Roll of Honour: War Casualties 1965 – 1980
The 38
Anglo Boer War Diaries of Jan Geldenhuys

Internet Links

Peysoft Publishing:
Lulu Spotlight Page 1 of 4:
Rhodesian Air Force Operations: http://www.lulu.com/shop/preller-geldenhuys/rhodesian-air-force-operations/paperback/product-21923866.html
The 38 : http://www.lulu.com/shop/preller-geldenhuys/the-38/paperback/product-22031512.html
Anglo-Boer War Diaries of Geldenhuys:
http://www.lulu.com/shop/preller-geldenhuys/anglo-boer-war-diaries-of-jan-geldenhuys/paperback/product-21966928.html
Rhodesia-Zimbabwe Roll of Honour: War Casualties 1965 – 1980:
http://www.lulu.com/shop/preller-geldenhuys/rhodesia-zimbabwe-roll-of-honour-war-casualties-1965-to-1980/ebook/product-21812978.html

Plus, several **eBooks – many costs free**: -
http://www.lulu.com/shop/preller-geldenhuys/rhodesian-air-force-operations/ebook/product-21831918.html

http://www.lulu.com/shop/preller-geldenhuys/rhodesia-zimbabwe-roll-of-honour-war-casualties-1965-to-1980/ebook/product-21812978.html

INDEX